P9-EFG-120

THE DEVELOPMENT OF CHILDREN'S CONCEPTS OF CAUSAL RELATIONS

UNIVERSITY OF MINNESOTA
THE INSTITUTE OF CHILD WELFARE
MONOGRAPH SERIES NO. XIII

THE DEVELOPMENT OF CHILDREN'S CONCEPTS OF CAUSAL RELATIONS

BY

JEAN MARQUIS DEUTSCHE

PSYCHOLOGIST, DELINQUENCY DIVISION
OF THE CHILDREN'S BUREAU

GREENWOOD PRESS, PUBLISHERS
WESTPORT, CONNECTICUT

Library of Congress Cataloging in Publication Data

Deutsche, Jean Marquis, 1910-
    The development of children's concepts of
causal relations.

    Reprint of the ed. published by the University of
Minnesota Press, Minneapolis, which was issued as no. 13
of Monograph series of the Institute of Child Welfare,
University of Minnesota.
    Based on the author's thesis, University of Minnesota,
1935.
    Bibliography: p.
    Includes index.
    1. Child study. 2. Reasoning (Psychology)
3. Mental tests. I. Title. II. Series: Minnesota.
University. Institute of Child Development and Welfare.
Monograph series ; no. 13.
LB1117.D47 1975   155.4'13   71-142312
ISBN 0-8371-5900-8

Originally published in 1937 by The University of Minnesota
Press, Minneapolis

Reprinted with the permission of The University of Minnesota
Press

Reprinted in 1975 by Greenwood Press,
a division of Williamhouse-Regency Inc.

Library of Congress Catalog Card Number 71-142312

ISBN 0-8371-5900-8

Printed in the United States of America

FOREWORD

Psychology is often accused of having strayed far from the field indicated in the derivation and original meaning of the phrase — "the science of mind." Of late psychologists have concentrated their attention on observable and measurable *behavior* and have neglected the classic problem of the nature of thinking, which was of such primary concern in an earlier day. Recently, under the stimulation of Koehler's researches on problem-solving in apes and Piaget's studies of children's logical processes, a new interest has arisen in the nature of thinking, and new techniques have been developed.

The present monograph records a skillfully devised and well-controlled investigation of the development of children's thinking. In Mrs. Deutsche's group test the children were allowed to write down in their own words answers to questions arising out of simple scientific demonstrations and to questions concerning natural phenomena which could not be so easily demonstrated. The multiple-choice answer method was considered and rejected, since it might tend to force the child's answers into categories provided by the examiners. The group method was employed rather than the individual examination method because it permitted the use of a larger number of subjects, thus increasing the validity of the observations and reducing the errors of sampling.

Piaget's pioneer work was used as a point of departure. Mrs. Deutsche, however, found only four of Piaget's seventeen types of causal thinking in large enough frequencies to warrant further analysis. She also found fewer non-naturalistic explanations than Piaget reports, and no evidence for the validity of his analysis of the development of causal thinking into stages.

The large number of children tested in this study made possible the calculation of age and sex trends in the development of children's concepts of causal relations, also of the trends of scores in relation to socio-economic status, intelligence, and school grade. The quantified scores have also been related to the number of words used in the children's answers. Particularly striking are the experimenter's findings that the majority of children's answers to questions about natural phenomena are materialistic in character, and

v

that answers of this type tend to be given in most cases even by children of kindergarten age. This would seem to indicate that, while children may enjoy fairy tales, tricks, and magic, they do not, in general, accept such explanations of events in the real world.

This is a profoundly interesting study in a field which, as the author says, has been too largely neglected in our preoccupation with the less complicated problems of human behavior. Mrs. Deutsche's lucid and graphic description of her experiment, and her numerous suggestions for further work along similar lines, make her monograph invaluable to anyone engaged in the investigation of children's thinking, or contemplating further work.

JOHN E. ANDERSON
Director, Institute of Child Welfare
University of Minnesota

ACKNOWLEDGMENTS

To Dr. John E. Anderson, who, as chairman of the committee, gave constant direction, assistance, and encouragement, and to Dr. Florence L. Goodenough, whose advice and cooperation were most helpful.

To the principals and teachers who cooperated in the testing program, and to the graduate students who assisted with the ratings.

J. M. D.

CONTENTS

THE DEVELOPMENT OF CHILDREN'S CONCEPTS
OF CAUSAL RELATIONS

I. INTRODUCTION

One of the most interesting and most important problems of psychology is the nature of thinking. Yet in the fields of both adult and child psychology, the higher mental processes have been neglected, whereas the simpler and less complicated problems have been the center of attention.

The scarcity of research on children's thinking, and our consequent limited knowledge of the subject, are not to be explained by a lack of interest in the problem, nor by a lack of appreciation of its importance, but rather by the extreme difficulty of formulating experimental methods for investigation which meet the needs of the problem and will help us in answering our questions.

The present investigation is concerned with the nature and development of children's concepts of causal relations — one phase of children's thinking. An understanding of the larger problem — how children think, and what factors are important in the development of child thought — will be reached only through further investigations of its various aspects.

The Problem

The work of Jean Piaget has aroused much interest in the nature of children's thought processes, with special reference to logical thinking and reasoning, and has stimulated valuable research within the past decade. As a pioneer worker in the field, Piaget contributed a technique for attacking these problems and a considerable insight into their nature. In spite of criticism of his methods, and the accumulating evidence against many of his results and conclusions, his research is still the point of departure for investigations in this field.

Using the individual testing method, Piaget (30) arrived at a systematized classification of children's concepts of causality including seventeen types of causal explanation representing three stages of development. The first two stages are precausal, whereas the third, appearing at about seven or eight years, and involving the mechanical type of explanation, is more truly causal. These stages of causal thinking are tied up with the progress from realism to objectivity, from egocentrism to socialization in the child.

Piaget's researches, as well as those of others succeeding him in the field, suggest the following problems for consideration:

1. What is the nature of the development of causal reasoning in the child? Does causal thinking develop in stages? Is it saltatory, or is there a gradual development in reasoning? Are certain stages (or degrees) in the development of causal reasoning characteristic of certain ages, or is there great overlapping between ages? Is there a general factor of reasoning, i. e., do children tend to give causal explanations of the same general level for all questions of causality, or is the level of the explanation specific to the particular question?

2. What is the value of Piaget's classification of causal thinking into seventeen types? Is this a valid classification? Are the types adequate and representative? Is it possible to use this classification to advantage? How do the stages, as outlined by Piaget, check with quantitative data such as are found in this study?

3. What relationships do outside factors bear to the development of causal thinking? Specifically, what is the relationship to causal thinking of factors such as language, sex, intelligence, and socio-economic status? Of what importance is the effect of schooling and specific instruction upon the kinds of causal explanations children give?

4. Is there evidence which will answer the question of the relative importance of maturation (stages determined biologically) and experience in determining the concepts of a given child?

REVIEW OF THE LITERATURE

Since so much of the experimental work on children's logicality, reasoning, etc., receives its impetus from Piaget, a brief summary of his procedures and conclusions should be considered first.

Using the individual interview method, Piaget (30) studied children's explanations of movement and of machines, and the relationship between ability to predict a given effect and ability to explain its cause. By direct questioning, sometimes with experiments or demonstrations, Piaget investigated ideas concerning the nature of air, the origin of wind and of breath, the movement of clouds and heavenly bodies, water currents and movements due to weight of objects dropped into the water, and ideas of force. By questioning and experiments he investigated the relation of prediction to explanation in the floating of boats, the effect on the level of water of dropping a stone in it, and the problem of shadows. By requiring drawings of a bicycle and by questions he studied children's understanding of the mechanisms of bicycles, steam engines, trains, motor cars, and airplanes. The number of children included in his study was apparently rather large, though the subjects were different for different parts of the study, and no data are given as to the number included in any particular phase.

As a result of these investigations, Piaget established seventeen distinct types of causal explanations, each characteristic of a different stage in the development of causal thinking. The first stage is characterized by psychological, phenomenistic, finalistic, and magical explanations; the second by artificialistic, animistic, and dynamic explanations, with magical forms decreasing; and the third by progressive disappearance of the preceding forms, and the appearance of more rational forms (reaction of surrounding medium, mechanical causality, causality by generation, substantial identification, schemas of condensation and rarefaction, atomistic composition, spatial explanation, and explanation by logical deduction). The first two periods are distinguished as precausal by the confusion of relations of a psychological or biological type in general with relations of a mechanical type. True concepts of causality are said not to appear until the third stage, at about seven or eight years.

According to Piaget, three processes characterize this evolution in causal thinking: (1) the desubjectification of causality (after 7 or 8 years), the child coming to distinguish between self and the universe; (2) recognition of a time sequence, as opposed to the immediacy of relations and the absence of intermediaries as found in explanations of 4- and 5-year-olds; and (3) the progressive reversibility of the systems of cause and effect, as opposed to the complete irreversibility of primitive forms of causality.

Simultaneously with the evolution of causal thinking, the child is proceeding from realism to objectivity, reciprocity, and relativity. That is, he recognizes what comes from himself and what from external reality as observed by anybody; he attributes the same value to others' points of view as to his own; and he does not assert that qualities or characters have independent substances or attributes. This progress from precausality to causality, and from realism to objectivity, Piaget ties up intimately with the progress from egocentrism to socialization. With the decline of egocentrism, the child begins to differentiate between inner and outer experience and to explain the world otherwise than in terms of himself.

Huang (19), limiting his experiments to phenomena outside the everyday experience of the child, reached conclusions different from

Piaget's. Using approximately 47 subjects between 4 and 10 years of age, and 11 college girls, he presented 14 experiments by the individual method. Of these, 3 were conjurer's tricks, 11 involved forces of nature, and 3 involved psychological factors affecting appearance (illusions). He found that nearly all the explanations were naturalistic physical concepts (though very simple), with few instances of psychological, finalistic, magical, moral, animistic, artificialistic, or mystical causality. This difference from Piaget's findings Huang attributes in part to the environment of the child and in part to the type of question asked. Piaget obtained most of his mystical explanations in reply to questions about the stars, the wind, etc. — a type that Huang did not include. Huang further concludes that some explanations are based wholly on knowledge. In these only ideation is involved. Others involve a cooperation of determinations from previous knowledge and suggestions from perceptual data. Still others involve mere contiguity.

Keen (23) studied the growth of concepts and reasoning concerning physical and psychological causation. By the use of a group-testing technique employing multiple choice answers to questions, and by individual testing, she succeeded in accumulating statistical evidence, based on a large number of cases, as to certain aspects of children's reasoning. By rating the answers of subjects in grades 6, 7, 10, and 11 and in the university, she obtained quantified scores for concepts of both physical and psychological causation. She finds evidence that reasoning is specific to the situation and not a general ability. The evidence lies in the low reliability of her test, due to the inequivalence of items; in the dependence of answers on verbalization, which suggests that reasoning is an organization of a number of specific traits of which an important one is the use of language; and in the influence of the content of the problems upon the score value of the answer. She finds no evidence of a difference between subjects of different ages as to the method used in formulating experiences, but does find differences in the amount of previous knowledge and experience upon which they have to draw and in the organization and systematization of that information. She discovers no evidence of consistent stages of development. Piaget's stages are represented, but in different proportions. She concludes that her evidence points to a gradual development of the reasoning process through more effective organization of concepts and through the growth of self-criticism. She finds very low correlation between concepts of psychological and of physical causation, especially at the lower age levels. A low correlation with intelligence is interpreted to mean that intelligence is compounded of a number of variables, of which reasoning of this type is one. Boys are found to be superior to girls in explanations of physical items, though the sex difference does not hold for psychological items.

Related studies on causality. — The data of Johnson and Josey (22), who repeated Piaget's (32) experiments on logical thinking, substantiate few of the latter's claims. They do not find animism, finalism, artificialism, etc., at 6 years. Instead, they find 6-year-old children socially minded, adopting hypotheses. They find no juxtaposition in reasoning or in drawings. Their children passed 33 of Piaget's tests where Piaget's children passed one. They find no egocentrism to hinder reasoning. Two possible explanations of the differences are offered: (1) that their group was slightly superior in intelligence and economic status, and (2) that perhaps the English language is superior to the French as an instrument for logical thinking.

Grigsby (11), working with preschool children, studied developmental trends in the concepts of time, space, part-whole, cause, discordance, and number. She used the clinical method, with automatic recording of conversations. With respect to the concept of cause, she finds there are four types of response at this age level: (1) causal relations somewhat removed from immediate experience; (2) expression of conclusions previously reached; (3) expression of ideas held by adults; and (4) irrelevant responses. Classifying her answers according to Piaget's seventeen types of causality, she finds results in agreement with his. Those problems lying close to the child's own perceptual or sensory experience are adequately expressed by some children from 2½ to 3½ years old, and by most of the older children. Concrete experiences not so closely touching sensory experience are expressed with greater difficulty. In regard to the dependence of concepts on vocabulary, Grigsby states that whereas understanding precedes verbal expression with most single words, this is not true where words are grouped to convey a given relation. Definite concepts lag far behind knowledge of words necessary for their expression. The same words are used for irrational expressions as for correct concepts.

Susan Isaacs (21) differs from Piaget in many conclusions regarding causal thinking in children. Her conclusions are based upon records and observations of children in the Malting House School for young children at Cambridge, England, where conditions were favorable for experimentation and inquiry on the part of the children, although no attempt was made to develop an interest in causality or to force explanations. Isaacs concludes that interest in mechanical causality, and ability to appreciate it, appear spontaneously much earlier than the middle years of childhood, the period indicated by Piaget; that the extent to which this interest is sustained and developed is partly a function of the social and physical environment; and that the conditions under which Piaget tried to measure interests and abilities were unfavorable to their manifestation. She argues against Piaget's maturational viewpoint (in terms of the "structure" of the child's mind at different ages), which is based upon a biological process of maturation of the nervous system. She would attribute to maturation only a limiting power, and would put greater emphasis upon the development of interest and the relation of increased experience to explanations of mechanical phenomena. Isaacs argues that Piaget's clinical method is inadequate for true measurement because of the nature of the questions involving actual knowledge, the suggestive power of the questions, and the intellectual disadvantage which the method gives to children. Her experience is that whereas children do not always function at the level of clear understanding, and sometimes exhibit modes of thought that are egocentric and syncretic, they are capable of clear spontaneous formulations. These, she maintains, can be observed only in natural situations, not in an artificial setup.

Becher (2) questioned 76 school children, aged 5 to 14, to determine their understanding of various fundamental concepts such as sickness, death, mind, etc. The findings were classified into types which showed a fairly definite developmental sequence, with four principal states: (1) if-when thinking, a statement of events and consequences; (2) religious and fairy tale theories; (3) magical theories; and (4) realistic theories.

Children were asked by Illge (20) to name certain things incomprehensible to them. Questions from this list were given to 12- and 13-year-olds; their answers covered a wide range, from explanations depending on magic to explanations which were scientifically correct.

Zawerska (41), using three demonstration experiments (two of which were used in the present investigation), studied the explanations of natural phenomena given by 218 children 9 to 11 years old. Group tests were used, as well as individual tests of 24 subjects. Zawerska found four types of response: (1) explanation by the succession in time of particular events; (2) animistic and dynamic explanations based on primitive beliefs; (3) mechanical explanations depending on series of reciprocal actions; and (4) explanations based on modern scientific concepts. He found that the fourth type, scientific concepts, was related to environment (town or country) and to the degree of well-being in the immediate social environment. A striking number of explanations were based on the idea of gravity.

Decroly (8) investigated the evolution of chromatic concepts up to the age of 4½ years; the development of notions of quality, time, age, growth, old age, objective and subjective values, stages of interest in animals and origin of things, and forms of competition; and certain aspects of the development of graphic aptitude in children up to 6 years.

The thinking of abnormal children was studied by Sander (34). Children in special classes and in a control group were told stories which they were to finish by drawing a series of illustrations. The continuation of the story required a recognition of the mechanical effect of the previous setup. The abnormal children mentioned the mechanical implications more rarely than emotionally colored consequences such as flight or punishment. The normal children interpreted the stories from various points of view, but the abnormal saw only one possible interpretation and retained this in their conclusions.

Hazlitt (14) attacks Piaget's assumption that thinking can be identified with ability to express oneself verbally and that the matter of thought has little effect on the process of thought. Basing her conclusions upon experiments in which children recognize exceptions and in which they find a common object, Hazlitt concludes that children can see relations at a very early age. She suggests that the egocentrism noted by Piaget is the result of lack of experience in seeing relations in the environment. She finds that adults make the same mistakes as children when dealing with unfamiliar material, and concludes that Piaget's picture of the difference between adult and childish thinking is due to an overvaluation of verbal expressions as a measure of thinking and to an exaggerated idea of the logicality of adult thought.

Further evidence of the effect of difficulty upon the type of response to questions is offered by Abel (1). Working with college students, Abel repeated with adults the experiments of Piaget on verbal understanding between children (32), using material of the same difficulty for adults as was Piaget's material for children 6 and 7 years old. The technique was that of telling a story which the child then reproduced for another child, who in turn explained it to the investigator. Piaget had reported a large degree of juxtaposition, reversal of order, and syncretism. These same forms of illogicality were found in adults. Abel concludes that for every normal person some compulsory stimulus-situation requiring logical thought will reveal limitations of memory and understanding of communication through verbal channels, and will force him to unsynthetic or prelogical modes of thought. An article by two parents (37), in which the diary record of questions and scientific interests of a preschool boy are analyzed, reports that the child gives animistic explanations of things beyond his comprehension and of matters about which he cannot experiment, but that he consistently gives causal explanations when he can experiment, when he is interested, and when the matter is within his range of understanding.

Raspe (33) had children observe experiments on contrast phenomena, geometrical optical illusions, images and simple reactions, and give their explanations of the phenomena. Herzfeld and Wolf (18) performed experiments on curiosity and theory-making and found three types of reasoning: (1) mythical, (2) magical, and (3) realistic. The realistic type comprised 49 per cent of the theories advanced at 6 years, 67 per cent at 7 years, 80.5 per cent at 8 years, and 96 per cent at 9 years. The conclusion was reached that realistic explanations predominate by 7 years of age. Zeininger (42) experimented with third-grade children to obtain their explanations of tadpoles, wind, rain, clouds, etc. His data support those of O. Kroh, whom he quotes, in that they emphasize the role of experience. At 6 years, if the subject matter is within the sphere of the child's experience, his explanation is realistic. Even at 11 and 12 years, children do not give realistic explanations if the subject matter is outside their experience.

Winch (40) in an experimental study of reasoning in school children reports a high correlation between reasoning ability (as measured by finding flaws in statements) and age; an increasing superiority of boys with age; and a high correlation with school placement, which is interpreted to mean that reasoning ability is highly correlated with intelligence. Bedell (3), studying the ability of children to recall and to generalize items of general science material (multiple choice technique), finds that boys excel girls in the ability to generalize, but that there is no sex difference in ability to recall. Burt (4), who has standardized tests of reasoning, states that he has shown that of all the tests proposed for the measurement of intelligence, those involving higher mental processes, especially reasoning, vary most closely with intelligence. He finds the correlation of reasoning with intelligence to be .64 to .78 within a single school grade.

Harrison (13) has attempted to determine the relation of maturation, training, and experience to the development of concepts of time. Working with 160 children from kindergarten through the third grade, he found seven degrees of understanding of words related to time (taken from language studies), ranging from complete comprehension of the general idea and specific facts to complete lack of understanding, no response, or "don't know." The degree of understanding of these concepts correlates .66 with school grade, .70 with mental age, and .58 with chronological age. The conclusion is that concepts of time are more closely related to inner maturation than to training and experience, although, of course, knowledge of the specific facts is dependent on training.

In contrast to Harrison, Peterson (27) concludes, from a study of the ability of elementary and secondary school children to generalize, that schooling is more closely related to such ability than is intelligence, as we measure it. Twenty problems involving a first-class lever were utilized. No correlation was found between either age and ability to solve these problems, or between intelligence and ability, when school grade was held constant. There was a positive correlation between grade and ability to solve, however, when age and intelligence were partialed out. Harrison also found slight sex differences favoring boys in ability to solve problems involving a general principle.

Social concepts of children were studied by Shaffer (35), who used two techniques: (1) free expression, in which the word was read and the child wrote what it meant to him, and (2) personal interview. There were two groups of subjects; with one the free expression method was used first and the personal interview second, with the other the reverse order. Of interest from the standpoint of method are the following findings: correlation between results of the personal interview followed by free expression, .67; free expression followed by personal interview, .50. Corrected for attenuation these coefficients become .74 and .55, respectively. The free expression method correlates .56 with a ten-item multiple choice test and .54 with a 32-element true-false test. The conclusion is that the group test method brings out as much information as the personal interview method.

Testing the suggested parallel between what anthropologists call animism in primitives and the spontaneous thought of children, Mead (26) studied children of the Admiralty Islands, utilizing observations, drawings, interpretations of ink blots, and direct questioning in an attempt to provoke animistic responses from these primitive children. She was unable to discover any tendency toward animistic thought. Rather, she discovered a negativism to explanations in animistic terms and a preference for cause-and-effect explanations. Mead concludes that animism cannot be explained in terms of intellectual immaturity.

A few studies involving problem solving and concept formation are of interest in connection with this study and will be reviewed here, though no attempt will be made to review the entire literature on the subject.

Heidbreder (15, 16) has compared children and adults in problem-solving situations with respect to their methods of attack and the reasons given for their reactions. She finds that reasons are much more readily elicited from adults than from children, with a sharp dividing line at about 5 or 6 years; that general ability to solve problems and responsiveness to them increase with age; that certain situations can be counted on to produce the thought response as opposed to reflex, emotional, or habitual behavior; that there is a gradual emergence of a general form or pattern of procedure that becomes more definite but never rigid; that there are age differences in reasons given; that reasons may be formed in a series which constitutes an objectively determined maturity scale; that there is, however, a tremendous overlapping of reasons between age groups; and that the objective situation influences both the quality and the number of the reasons, although here again age differences assert themselves over and above this.

Studying the evolution of concepts in adults through association of nonsense syllables with given situations, Heidbreder (17) found that concepts evolved more easily from pictured than from verbal material; that concepts were often used with consistent correctness though the subject was unable to formulate them verbally; and that instances of both sudden and gradual concept formation occurred throughout the experiment.

A problem-solving situation used by Chant (5) in an objective experiment on reasoning in adults led to the conclusion that two methods were utilized for solution: (1) an interpretive approach, in which answers were derived from previously established associations and (2) an analytical approach, in which answers were derived from direct comparison of the material. It was found that the adults reverted to the interpretive approach whenever the previous association was obvious.

Guillet (12) studied the growth of a child's concept by his definitions of words at 4, 7, and 10 years. Arbitrarily assigned scores showed that the value of the performance of the 4-year-old was but 30 per cent and that of the 7-year-old but 52 per cent of the performance of the 10-year-old child. The number of words used at 4 was 25 per cent and at 7 was 38 per cent of the number used at 10. Guillet concludes that there is much greater growth of concepts and power of expression between 7 and 10 years than between 4 and 7 years.

Summary of the literature. — A review of the literature on children's concepts of causal relations and certain related problems leaves us with little understanding of the nature of the development of this function.

We find investigations supporting Piaget's stages of development — in which types of answers are found at rather specific ages. But the preponderance of the studies report great overlapping between age groups, and a scatter of different kinds of answers throughout the age range. Some investigators agree with Piaget in his classification of types of causal thinking and substantiate his findings, whereas others discover little evidence to support his age relationships and his claim as to the prevalence of precausal thinking in younger children. There is conflicting evidence as to the relative roles of innate factors and experiential factors, or direct training. Little evidence exists as to the extent of sex differences or the role of intelligence, socio-economic status, etc., in determining the level of the child's thinking. We have evidence for and against (mainly against) real differences between the thinking of children and adults. Most of the evidence suggests that degree of difficulty determines the kind of response.

We find few studies conducted on such a scale that statistical evidence for or against certain propositions can be presented. The control of samples is very poor — a rather important point, as is shown by Keen (23) and by the present study.

DIFFERENCES BETWEEN THIS STUDY AND PREVIOUS STUDIES

The major difference between this study and previous ones lies in their varying testing techniques. The group-testing technique here employed has an advantage over the multiple choice test in that the child's own individual interpretation is obtained and his answers are not forced into preconceived categories. It has advantages over the individual testing technique, also, in that it permits the testing of a large number of cases. Thus statistical analysis of the data may be made, and sampling errors avoided. The method allows for statistical analysis of the development of causal thinking and for determination of the effect of related factors such as sex, intelligence, school grade, and socio-economic status.

In this study two types of analysis of children's causal thinking — quantitative and qualitative — have been made. Through these two analyses, comparison and checks of previous experiments may be made and the relationship between the two aspects of causal thinking studied. The qualitative analysis of children's answers has been carried farther than by Piaget or by other investigators. Further classifications of the data were made in order to reveal new relationships and test certain hypotheses.

II. THE EXPERIMENT

Preliminary Work

The selection of questions of causality for the children to answer was an important problem. There were quite definite criteria that the questions must satisfy:

1. The questions based on demonstrations of experiments (for Form I) had to be practicable for performance in the schoolroom. The apparatus involved had to be small enough to be transported easily; the action of the experiment had to be simple enough for the children to distinguish what happened; and the apparatus had to be large enough and simple enough so that children all over the room could observe the facts of the experiment without difficulty.

2. It was desirable that many of the questions should have been used previously in studies of causality, in order that the findings could be compared with those of other investigators.

3. The problems involved in the questions had to be definite — that is, the children must be able to understand clearly what it was they were expected to explain.

4. It was desirable that questions elicit answers with a considerable range of completeness in order that age relationships could be observed. In order to get answers from all the children and answers with a wide range of adequacy as explanations, the questions had to be neither too hard for the young children nor too easy for the older children.

5. The questions necessarily had to be such as to provoke some kind of reply from most of the children. A large percentage of omissions would have precluded any possibility of analysis.

The first step in selecting questions was to survey the literature on the subject of causality, noting the various experiments and questions that had been used by others. This list was then supplemented in various ways — by a careful search for suggestions in an elementary physics and an elementary chemistry text, by a search through catalogues of magic and trick equipment, and by the use of imagination. This initial list of suggestions was cut down by eliminating those questions which seemed unlikely to meet all requirements. There remained 14 questions with experiments and 23 questions without.

A preliminary trial of these questions was made with adults (graduate students in the Institute of Child Welfare). The 14 questions with experiments were tried with a group of seven adults. They were instructed to answer the questions on the phenomena as adequately as they could, and then to append suggestions or criticism of the whole procedure. The 23 questions without experiments (Form II) were mimeographed and given to 14 adult students with instructions to answer them as adequately as possible, to make suggestions and criticisms, and to indicate which questions were the hardest and which the easiest.

A similar preliminary tryout was made with children the age of those upon whom it was proposed to make the final investigation. Twelve children, from 8 to 15 years, came to the Institute for a demonstration of Form I. The experiments were performed and the children were requested to answer the questions in the spaces provided on the blanks. Six of these same children later answered the preliminary draft of Form II.

The results of the preliminary trials were very satisfactory, and made possible a selection of items for the final forms. The items proposed for Form I all proved quite usable, eliciting a range of answers on each question and responses from nearly all the subjects. Because of the length of the form, however, three items were eliminated. The questions designed for Form II elicited less complete and varied answers. A tabulation was made of the number of times each question was mentioned as being hard or easy, the number of times each was omitted, and the variety of answers given. Nine questions were finally dropped from this form.

FINAL FORMS OF THE TEST

The instructions and directions used in the administration of the first form of the experiment are given below.

General directions.—Experimenter says, "This is not a test that I am giving you today. I can't mark you right or wrong on these questions. I just want to find out what you think about these experiments. First write your name, grade, age at last birthday, and what your father does.

"Now I am going to do some experiments. We'll watch and see what happens. Then you write in the spaces on the paper what you think makes it happen—why it happens that way—what causes it. Write the very best answer you can give, but don't take very long to write it."

1. CANDLE IN JAR
   Apparatus: Candle, glass jar.

Directions: Light candle. Cover with jar.

Comments: "I have a candle here that I am going to light. See! It is burning nicely. Now, I'm going to put this jar over the candle. It doesn't touch it at all. What happens? The candle went out! What made it stop burning? Why won't it burn in the jar? *Why does the candle go out?*"*

2. PENNY IN BOX

Apparatus: Penny. Cardboard box top with string attached to each corner.

Directions: Hold box upside down to show that penny falls out. Then whirl vertically.

Comments: "I have a top to a box here, with strings on it so it will stay flat. Now, I'll put a penny in the middle of the box. What would happen if I turned the box upside down? The penny would fall out, wouldn't it? See! Now watch. I'm going to turn the box around and around. The penny is still in it! Why does the penny stay in the box? *Why doesn't the penny fall out?*"

3. LEVEL OF WATER

Apparatus: Beaker partly filled with water. Large pebble.

Directions: Put pebble in water.

Comments: "I have a glass of water here, filled with water up to here [point]. Now I'm going to put a pebble in. Now look! The water comes up to here now [point]. What makes the water come up this far now? *Why does the water come up higher when I put the pebble in?*"

4. BLOCK DROPPING

Apparatus: Small wooden block.

Directions: Drop from height of two feet above the table.

Comments: "I have just an ordinary piece of wood here, painted green. Listen when I drop the block on the table! Did you hear the noise? What causes the noise? *What makes the noise when the block falls?*"

5. CHANGING COLOR OF LIQUIDS

Apparatus: Beaker of water. Eye dropper. Small bottles of bromcresol green, methyl red, hydrochloric acid.

Directions: Add a few drops of bromcresol green to the water, then add hydrochloric acid. Add a few drops of methyl red to the water in the other beaker, then add hydrochloric acid.

Comments: "I have a glass of plain water here. I'm going to add some of this blue stuff to make the water all blue. Now watch the water. I'm going to put in just a little bit of this stuff without any color. What happens to the blue water? It is yellow now, isn't it? Now

* The italicized questions are the ones which appeared on the mimeographed sheet on which the subjects wrote their explanations.

watch again. In this water I'm going to put some of this, and make the water yellow. Now, I'll pour in some of this stuff that hasn't any color. Watch! What color is it this time? It's red! Why does the blue change to yellow and the yellow to red? *What makes the water change color when I pour in some of this colorless stuff?*"

6. BULB ON TUBE

Apparatus: Beaker of colored water. Hydrometer.

Directions: Repeatedly draw water into hydrometer.

Comments: "I have a tube here, with a piece of rubber on the end that is hollow. Watch the water come up in the tube. I squeeze the top and then let it out, and the water comes right up in the tube. Why does it do this? How does this happen? *What makes the water go up in the tube when I let go of the bulb?*"

7. TEETER-TOTTERS

Apparatus: Two small teeter-totters, one with fulcrum in the middle, one with it definitely toward one end. Three small blocks of equal size and weight, one block that is larger and heavier.

Directions: Demonstrate the equal-armed teeter-totter with equal blocks. Put third block on long arm of second teeter-totter. Show two equal blocks will not balance. Replace small block with big one on short arm of second teeter-totter.

Comments: "I have two teeter-totters here. Now here are two blocks that weigh just the same. If I put one of them on each end of this teeter-totter, it will balance. See, each end is off the table. On this other teeter-totter, if I put these two blocks on the ends, one end goes 'way down. It won't balance. But if I put this big block on this end, it will balance. Why won't this teeter-totter balance with the two little blocks? *Why do I have to put a big block on one end to make this teeter-totter balance?*"

8. MIXED LIQUIDS

Apparatus: Closed test tube containing water, carbon tetrachloride, and methyl red.

Directions: Mix liquids thoroughly, then stand tube on end.

Comments: "I have a tube here with two liquids in it. One is just plain water, and one is red. I mix them all up, so that it is all red. Now, when I stand this up and let it stay that way for a minute, what happens? All the red liquid is at the top and the colorless stuff is at the bottom. Why do they separate like this? *Why does the colored liquid separate from the colorless liquid?*"

9. PAPER OVER JAR

Apparatus: Glass jar partly filled with water. Unglazed paper.

Directions: Cover jar with paper and invert.

Comments: "I'm going to fill this jar with water, and put a piece of paper over the top. What would happen if I turned the jar upside down? Would the water fall out? Let's see. No, it doesn't, does it? What makes the water stay in the jar? *Why don't the paper and water fall out of the jar?*"

10. MUSICAL INSTRUMENT

   Apparatus: Horn, with keys, which has reeds.

   Directions: Play horn, making finger movements obvious.

   Comments: "I have a horn here. I'm going to play on it for you. Watch what I do to make it play. I blow, and move my fingers on the keys. Listen to this note [high]. Now listen to this one [low]. And this [intermediate]. What makes these sound different when I blow? What makes the different sounds? Why does it sound high one time and low the next? *Why does it make different sounds when I push different keys?*"

11. WATER LEVEL OF CONNECTED TUBES

   Apparatus: Connected glass tubes, with turn-stop in connecting tube. Water.

   Directions: Put water into one tube. Turn stopper.

   Comments: "Here are two glasses, connected so that the water can go from one to the other. But I can keep the water from going into both sides by turning this stopper this way. Let's fill this side. There is no water on this other side now. Now, we will turn the stopper and see what happens. The water comes 'way up here on this side now! Why does the water come up just as far on this side as on the other? *Why does the water run up hill in the little tube?*"

The directions and questions which were included in the second form of the test are given below.

Directions: "Answer these questions the very best you can, and as quickly as possible."

1. What makes the wind blow?
2. What makes the snow?
3. Why do balloons go up in the air?
4. Two men both named Carl Jenkins were killed at four o'clock the same day, one in San Francisco, one in Kansas City, and both were killed in an automobile accident. How do you explain this?
5. What makes the rainbow after the rain?
6. What makes airplanes able to stay up in the air?
7. What makes frost on the windows in wintertime?
8. Why do boats float on top of the water instead of sinking?
9. A man built a barn, and it was hit by lightning. He built it again three times, and each time lightning struck it and it burned. How do you explain why it was struck by lightning four times?
10. What makes shadows?
11. What causes thunder?
12. How is it you can see yourself when you look into a mirror?

Questions which were eliminated. — The three items eliminated from Form I were the following:

1. SPINNING TOP

   Apparatus: Top.

   Directions: Spin, then let it fall. Repeat.

   Comments: "This is just an ordinary top like you have played with. I am going to spin it. What makes it spin? If I just hold it up and let go, it falls over. If I spin it, it stays standing up for quite a while. What makes it stand up on the little end, and now fall? *Why doesn't the top fall over when I spin it?*"

2. WATER IN TUBE WITH FINGER

   Apparatus: Small glass tube. Water in beaker.

   Directions: Fill tube partly with water. Hold finger over top. Release water. Refill.

   Comments: "This is a piece of glass with a hole up through the middle — just a glass tube. I'm filling it part way with water. Now, when I hold it up, the water doesn't fall out. Why doesn't the water fall out? If I take my finger off, it all runs out. I fill it again, and hold my finger over the end, and it stays in. *Why does the water fall out when I take my finger off?*"

3. MAGNET

   Apparatus: Magnet, nail.

   Directions: Pick up nail with magnet, repeatedly.

   Comments: "See this horseshoe-shaped piece I have in my hand? It is a magnet. If I put it near this nail, what happens? The nail is lifted right up. We'll try again. *What makes the nail go up when I lift the magnet?*"

The question of the spinning top was eliminated because it called forth answers which fell within a narrow range; the water held in the small tube by the finger was omitted because the apparatus was small and the phenomenon so inconspicuous that it was difficult for the children to see what happened, and because there were too many items involving pressure; the magnet and nail question was omitted because the answers fell within a rather narrow range and because there were several omissions.

The questions eliminated from the preliminary form of Form II were the following:

1. What makes the waves on the lake?
2. Why do clouds move across the sky?
3. What makes water boil?
4. What makes the sun seem to move across the sky?
5. Why is the grass green?

6. A man in Denver has a chicken with three legs. How do you explain this?

7. On Friday the thirteenth a boy broke a window, lost his favorite knife, and fell from a tree and broke his leg. How do you explain why all this happened?

8. A man away from home dreamed that his mother was dead, and went home the next night and found her dying. How do you explain this?

9. Two boys, 20 years old, who were twins, hadn't seen each other for ten years. They both committed murder during the same week, one in Germany, one in France. How do you explain this?

The first four of these questions were omitted because nearly all the explanations were identical. One question (Why is the grass green?) was eliminated because it was too difficult, and no answers were at all adequate. The last four questions were dropped because they merely duplicated the purpose of two questions (4 and 10) which were retained in the final form.

Administration of the Tests

Form I of the questionnaire was administered to the children in grades 3 through 8 of Longfellow School, St. Paul, on two successive days in November, 1933; to the children in grades 3 through 6 of Lincoln School, Brainerd, and to two sections each of grades 7B, 7A, 8B, and 8A of the junior high school, Brainerd, on two successive days in January, 1934. Form II was given to these same children in Brainerd two days after the first form. The Brainerd testing was all completed within a one-week interval. The schedule for testing was arranged so as to permit as little opportunity as possible for discussing the questions outside of school.

The tests were given to one schoolroom at a time. After being introduced by the teacher, the experimenter explained the general nature of the project. In administering Form I, the apparatus was arranged, the children were instructed to fill out the information at the top of the blank, and the experimenter then proceeded with the general directions and demonstrations outlined above. Sufficient time was allowed after each demonstration for all the children to complete their writing. The time required for completion of the form was approximately 35 minutes. In giving Form II, the experimenter explained that there were similar questions to be answered, without any demonstrations. In grades 3 through 6 the questions were read aloud by the investigator, and sufficient time was allowed for the writing of answers before the next question was read. In grades 7 and 8 the children were allowed to work independently at their own rate of speed. Help in spelling was given in the lower grades. No questions were permitted to be asked aloud, but when a child raised his hand, either the teacher or the experimenter went to him and answered his question quietly. This rule of silence was made hard-and-fast to prevent the suggestion of answers. The motivation factor was supplied by the tests themselves, which aroused a surprising amount of interest. The attention of the children was held completely, and there was every evidence from their reactions that they were cooperating fully. The experimenter was besieged after school and on the street by children asking questions about the phenomena. Further evidence that the motivation was adequate is found in the completeness of the responses. The number of omissions and incomplete responses was very low.

TABLE I. — SEX AND AGE DISTRIBUTION OF TOTAL GROUP TESTED

Sex	Age in Years								Total
	8	9	10	11	12	13	14	15–16	
Boys . . .	22	52	59	47	77	83	27	14	381
Girls . . .	30	45	54	62	69	58	19	14	351
Total. .	52	97	113	109	146	141	46	28	732

DESCRIPTION OF SUBJECTS

Seven hundred thirty-two children between the ages of 8 and 16 years were tested. Seven hundred children took Form I of the test — 382 in the Longfellow School, St. Paul, including all the children in grades 3 through 8, and 318 Brainerd children, including grades 3 through 6 in the Lincoln School and two sections each of 7B, 7A, 8B, and 8A in the junior high school. Three hundred thirty-five children from the Brainerd groups took Form II of the test. The sexes were distributed almost equally on both forms, although there were slight variations from age to age. Three hundred sixty-one boys and 339 girls answered the questions on Form I; 164 boys and 171 girls answered the questions on Form II. Table 1 gives the sex distribution according to age. It will be seen that the proportion of girls is slightly higher at 8, 11, and 15–16 years than at other ages, but that the differences are slight.

In order to determine whether or not this group is representative of the whole population, the experimenter compared the socio-economic status of these children with that of the population as a whole. The Institute of Child Welfare revision (9) based on the Barr ratings of the Taussig scale was used to classify the subjects into occupational groups for the purpose of obtaining a measure of socio-economic status. The father's occupation was used when given in sufficient detail; the mother's, rated according to the scale for women, when her occupation alone was available. Socio-economic status ratings were possible for 651 of the 732 cases. Table 2 gives the distribution of cases falling in each occupational group at each age level.

TABLE 2. — OCCUPATIONAL CLASSIFICATION OF GROUP TESTED, ACCORDING TO AGE

Occupational Group	Age in Years								Total
	8	9	10	11	12	13	14	15–16	
I	6	9	3	6	17	9	0	0	50
II	9	6	20	15	19	17	3	2	91
III	14	30	22	25	43	29	9	6	178
IV	0	1	0	1	0	5	1	2	10
V	13	25	27	27	28	31	12	5	158
VI	1	7	8	12	14	21	12	5	80
VII	3	9	16	12	15	18	5	6	84

In this classification, Group I represents the professional class; Group II the managerial class; Group III the clerical, skilled trades, and retail business class; Group IV, farmers; Group V, the semi-skilled trades, minor clerical, and minor business class; Group VI, the slightly skilled class; and Group VII, the laboring class.

An inspection of Table 2 reveals that there are fewer children in the upper socio-economic groups at the higher age levels than at the lower age levels; and that there are larger numbers in the lower socio-economic groups at the higher ages than at the lower ages. This is to be accounted for by the fact that the larger proportion of cases at the upper age levels was from the junior high school at Brainerd, which draws from a population slightly below average in socio-economic status, whereas the larger proportion of cases at the lower age levels were obtained in a St. Paul school that draws from a better than average section of the city. The extent of this tendency will be seen in Table 3, which presents the mean occupational status for each age group and for all ages, and also sex differences in socio-economic status.

TABLE 3. — MEAN OCCUPATIONAL STATUS OF GROUP TESTED,
ACCORDING TO AGE AND SEX *

Sex	Age in Years								All Ages
	8	9	10	11	12	13	14	15–16	
Boys . . .	3.26	3.65	3.53	3.40	3.26	3.57	3.96	....	3.52
Girls . . .	2.93	3.30	3.83	3.80	3.47	4.00	4.44	....	3.69
Both . .	3.06	3.49	3.68	3.62	3.35	3.75	4.17	4.27	3.60

* These ratings are based on the system of classification described on page 23, except that Group IV (farmers) was included with the class it most closely approximates (Group V). This group for purposes of calculation was called IV, and Groups VI and VII were called V and VI, respectively.

The drop in average socio-economic status from the 8-year to the 15–16-year group is, therefore, slightly more than one occupational class — approximately from the clerical, skilled trades, and retail business group to the semi-skilled occupations, minor clerical, and minor business group.

There is very little difference between the two sexes as to mean occupational status at the various age levels. On the whole, the girls' status is slightly lower than the boys', but the difference is exceedingly slight.

TABLE 4. — OCCUPATIONAL DISTRIBUTION OF EXPERIMENTAL
POPULATION COMPARED WITH THAT OF TYPICAL MALE
POPULATION IN MINNEAPOLIS

Occupational Group	Percentage of Experimental Group	Percentage of Male Population of Minneapolis *
I	7.7	4.2
II	14.0	10.0
III	27.3	22.9
IV	1.5	0.2
V	24.3	42.6
VI	12.3	7.6
VII	12.9	12.7

* Data on Minneapolis are based on the United States Census for 1930.

For the purpose of comparing the distribution of the experimental population with the distribution of the population as a whole, the percentage of parents falling in each occupational group was compared with the percentage of males in the general population falling in each group as determined by the 1930 census of Minneapolis (10). This criterion is not wholly adequate, since the experimental group is composed of residents of a small community as well as of a large one, but the criterion is the best available, and serves the purpose. The two lists of percentages are given in Table 4. An inspection of this table shows no wide divergence between the experimental group and the population as a whole with respect to occupational status, though there is a tendency for the experimental group to be of a somewhat higher status.

TABLE 5. — DISTRIBUTION OF AGE GROUPS ACCORDING TO SCHOOL GRADE

Grade	Age in Years							
	8	9	10	11	12	13	14	15–16
Grade 3	37	15	0	1	0	0	0	0
Grade 4	15	74	26	4	1	1	0	0
Grade 5	0	8	79	21	5	3	2	0
Grade 6	0	0	8	70	23	8	0	0
Grade 7	0	0	0	12	100	40	10	13
Grade 8	0	0	0	1	17	89	34	15
Mean grade . .	3.79	4.43	5.34	6.33	7.57	8.01	8.15	8.04

The distribution of cases according to age and school grade is presented in Table 5. It will be seen that between the ages of 9 and 12 the progress is approximately one grade each year, as would be expected. Between the ages of 8 and 9, however, and between ages from 12 up, it is less than one grade. This is explained by two facts. By not testing below the third grade, we have tested only the average or superior 8-year-old children, thereby raising the average grade for 8-year-olds. The upper limit is similarly distorted by a selection of cases. The average and superior 14- to 16-year-old children have left the eighth grade and entered senior high school, so that only a few remain in the eighth grade. If we assume what has been frequently demonstrated, that there is a considerable relationship between the intelligence of the child and his grade placement with respect to age, it seems likely that at the extremes of the age distributions our group is selected with respect to intelligence. Our 8-year-old group is very possibly superior to average 8-year-old children, and the 14- to 16-year-old groups are probably progressively inferior in intelligence to average children of these ages.

Such information relating to the intelligence of the children was obtained as was available in the files of the schools where the testing was done. No data were available on the intelligence of the children attending Lincoln School in Brainerd. Incomplete data were obtained on the Brainerd Junior High School subjects, including 93 IQ's based on the Kuhlmann-Anderson Intelligence Test, and 76 others based on the Army Alpha Test. Mental ages could be calculated for 49 of the Kuhlmann-Anderson cases and for all 76 Army Alpha cases. The data were likewise incomplete on the subjects from Longfellow School, St. Paul. Unit Aptitude quotients were obtained for 240 children, for all of whom mental age could be calculated; and achievement ratings were obtained for 91 cases. The number of IQ's based on any one test at a single age level is too small to determine the similarity of the different age groups as to intelligence.

TABLE 6. — PERCENTAGE DISTRIBUTION OF IQ'S, OBTAINED FROM
THREE INTELLIGENCE TESTS

IQ	Kuhlmann-Anderson		Army Alpha		Unit Aptitude	
	Number	Per Cent	Number	Per Cent	Number	Per Cent
60–69. . . .	1	1.1	0	0.0	3	1.2
70–79. . . .	0	0.0	1	1.3	6	2.5
80–89. . . .	10	10.8	6	7.9	15	6.2
90–99. . . .	21	22.6	8	10.5	62	25.8
100–09. . . .	33	35.5	18	23.7	79	32.9
110–19. . . .	16	17.2	24	31.6	62	25.8
120–29. . . .	8	8.6	12	15.8	9	3.8
130–39. . . .	4	4.3	4	5.3	4	1.7
140 and over .	0	0.0	3	3.9	0	0.0

Because there is no way in which the selection of cases for testing can be determined, and because the incompleteness of the data on intelligence is serious, no conclusions can be drawn as to the intellectual level of the experimental group. There is some evidence, however, that this is a relatively unselected group. Table 6, which gives the percentage distribution of IQ's obtained by the three different tests, reveals a fairly normal distribution of cases, with slightly heavier weighting of cases toward the upper extreme. Further evidence of this is found in the mean IQ as determined for each test. These means are presented in Table 7, with the mean for each sex given separately to show the comparative ratings of the two sexes. This table indicates that at least the cases tested are slightly above average in IQ, and that there is a tendency, though slight, for the girls tested to have higher intelligence quotients than the boys. No definite conclusions as to the group as a whole can be drawn from these incomplete data.

TABLE 7. — MEAN IQ'S FOR THE TWO SEXES, OBTAINED FROM THREE INTELLIGENCE TESTS

Sex	Mean IQ		
	Kuhlmann-Anderson	Army Alpha	Unit Aptitude
Boys	101.34	111.00	103.29
Girls	107.69	111.45	104.47
Both	104.89	111.23	103.75

Achievement ratings of 91 children corroborate the above findings. The percentages were as follows: very superior, 19.8 per cent; superior, 28.6 per cent; average, 39.6 per cent; inferior, 8.8 per cent; very inferior, 3.3 per cent. The girls were considerably superior to the boys. These data are entirely from Longfellow School, where the socio-economic status is higher than average.

To summarize: 732 children were included in this experiment, 700 of whom answered the questions on Form I and 335 the questions on Form II. The age range is from 8 to 16 years, with the greater proportion of the cases in the middle of the range. The socio-economic status of the younger children is slightly higher than that of the older children, and the socio-economic status of the group as a whole is slightly higher than that of the population of Minneapolis as determined by the 1930 census. The age-grade distribution is normal in the middle range, but indicates a selection of cases on the basis of intelligence at the extreme ages. Available data on intelligence are insufficient to determine the intellectual level of the group as a whole, but suggest that the group is of only slightly more than average intelligence.

TREATMENT OF THE DATA

Two types of analysis have been made of the data obtained on this experiment. One was quantified; the child's answers were evaluated in terms of the adequacy of the answer as a scientific explanation of the phenomenon; the other was a qualitative analysis in terms of the kinds of answers given, the types of approach used by the child, and the types of thinking involved.

The quantified scores, derived by weighted ratings, have been analyzed for reliability and consistency, and such factors studied as age relationships, sex differences, and the relationship between quantified scores and socio-economic status, school grade, and intelligence. A rough language measure, the number of words used in the replies, has been employed, and the reliability and consistency determined. The relationships between this measure and age, sex, socio-economic status, school grade, and intelligence, and the relationship between number of words used and the quantified scores have been found.

The qualitative analysis began with a direct application of Piaget's technique of classifying explanations into types of causal thinking. This technique was evaluated. Age, sex, and socio-economic trends in types of causal thinking were determined, for direct comparison with Piaget's findings. A further qualitative analysis of the explanations was made by means of a new sequence classification; this was devised and studied in its relationship to age, sex, and socio-economic status. A further analysis of one division of the sequence classification led to a materialistic sequence, which was analyzed in the same manner. This acted as a supplement to Piaget's classification and aided in testing certain hypotheses.

III. ANALYSIS OF QUANTIFIED SCORES

DERIVATION OF SCORES

A quantified scoring system for the answers to the various questions was much to be desired. A measure of the adequacy of the answers *as explanations of the phenomena involved* would give us a direct measure of the child's understanding of the problem, free from any philosophical implications as to logicality, etc. It would also give us an opportunity to study the development of such an understanding and its relationship to such other factors as sex, socio-economic status, and intelligence, and provide us with a measure to which correlational analysis might be applied.

Grouping of answers. — Since there were approximately twelve thousand answers to questions, it would have been entirely impracticable to deal with each answer individually in every analysis of the data. All answers to one question which were identical in expression or content were therefore grouped. It was found that certain answers were given with a high frequency, and that there was no very great variety of answers to any one question. The frequency within these groups covered a wide range — from several hundred to one — but it was necessary to make special cases of the individual answers in order to preserve the actual answers of the children.

The number of groups of answers to a question varied considerably from question to question. The answers to the question about the candle in the jar (Form I, question 1) were classified into 16 groups, whereas the answers to the question about water in connected tubes (Form I, question 11) required 35 groups for complete classification.

Quantified ratings. — Thirteen graduate students in the Institute of Child Welfare were requested to rate the answers, assigning an arbitrary score value to each of the typical answers. For example, on the question, "What makes the candle go out?" there were sixteen different answers, each of which was to be assigned a score value of from 0 to 7. The rating scale had eight points; a score of 7 represented a correct and complete answer; 6, very good; 5, good; 4, fair; 3, inadequate; 2, very inadequate; 1, entirely incorrect; and 0, no answer. A definition was furnished for each scale value, with the suggestion that the definitions might not fit each question, nor allow for the classification of each answer, and that the definitions were not to be adhered to strictly but to be taken merely as suggestions. The definitions were as follows:

7. *Correct answer.* — All essential principles mentioned or implied, and the right relationships explained.

6. *Very good.* — Slightly less than correct. Not *all* essential principles in right relations. Or incomplete explanation.

5. *Good.* — One principle and relation correct at least, but not necessarily the essential ones.

4. *Fair.* — Some sense of true relationship. Inadequate explanation of the relation.

3. *Inadequate.* — Principles inadequate or incorrect, or, relationships inadequately or incorrectly expressed.

2. *Very inadequate.* — Principles involved incorrect and inadequate, yet on the right track — i. e., appealing to proper agents, etc.

1. *Incorrect.* — Some answer, but entirely wrong in principles, relations, and agents.

0. Omitted, incomplete, "don't know," or incomprehensible.

The raters were reminded that this was to be an objective rating, that the answers were to be rated on their adequacy as an explanation of the phenomena, not as to their psychological value. The suggestion was made that there would not necessarily be an equal number of answers at each rating value. For example, for some questions there might be no perfect or 7 values; there might be many 3's and few 5's, etc.

In order to assure an understanding of the phenomena by the raters, a set of complete and accurate answers to the questions was furnished each rater. To obtain these, a graduate student in physics was enlisted to write the best explanations he could, from the standpoint of the physicist. These explanations were then corrected and approved by the head of the physics department. The revised explanations accompanied the rating slips.

Reliability of the ratings. — The reliability of the ratings was determined for each question by correlating the mean ratings of six judges with the mean ratings of six other judges. The uncorrected coefficients, as obtained for the ratings of each question, are found in Table 8. The agreement between the two groups of raters is strikingly close, and suggests that scores for individual answers based on the ratings of these judges are highly reliable.

Conversion to final scores. — The raw median rating value for each answer, while adequate for comparison of answers to a single question, does not assure us of comparable scores from question to question. A quantified score was desired which would permit comparison of findings on different questions. For this purpose a weighting scheme was devised, based on sigma score values. The procedure was as follows:

1. Median rating scale value for each answer was expressed in terms of its percentage of the perfect score (which in each case was 7).

TABLE 8. — CORRELATION BETWEEN MEAN QUANTIFIED RATINGS OF
ANSWERS MADE BY JUDGES

Form I			Form II		
Question	Number of Answers	Correlation	Question	Number of Answers	Correlation
Candle in jar	16	.964	Wind	30	.937
Penny in box	21	.939	Snow	31	.966
Level of water	26	.951	Balloons	25	.946
Block dropping	33	.949	Carl Jenkins	25	.985
Changing color of liq-			Rainbow.	28	.940
uids	22	.982	Airplanes	32	.953
Bulb on tube	30	.957	Frost	23	.977
Teeter-totters.	18	.981	Boats	31	.966
Mixed liquids.	28	.971	Barns	30	.960
Paper over jar	34	.937	Shadows	22	.900
Musical instrument . .	34	.953	Thunder	23	.976
Connected tubes . . .	35	.941	Mirror.	31	.867

2. This percentage value was then converted to the sigma score value corresponding to that percentage. The table used for this purpose was based on Thorndike's values.

3. The sigma value was then divided by 2; 46 was subtracted from this; and the remainder was divided by 10. The relative value of the scores was not altered by this manipulation, which had the advantage of giving small score values.

4. The final quantified score assigned to each answer was the nearest whole number to the score obtained.

There are two assumptions underlying this treatment of the rating that must be correct if such manipulation of the scores is to be justified: (1) that if we have a group in which the median ability to answer these questions falls at the median of the scale, the answers given will fall into a normal distribution from 0 to 7 and (2) that the distances between scale values are approximately equal.

There is no way of demonstrating that these assumptions are correct with respect to the data in question. It seems reasonable, however, to assume that, if we had a group without selection or truncation of the distribution, the answers would fall into a normal distribution with respect to their adequacy. In regard to the second criterion, the instructions to raters were so worded as to suggest that the distance between scale values should be equal. It is reasonable to suppose that the ratings were made with this in mind and that approximate equality was attained.

An illustration of the kind of treatment given to each question is presented below. First is given the correct explanation of "Why does the candle go out?" as it was explained to the judges. Following this are listed all the answers given by the children, with the quantified scores at which we arrived by the process outlined above.

Correct explanation of Form I, question 1. — Burning, more technically, combustion, is a process in which oxygen combines with some inflammable substance. The burning candle rapidly consumes all the oxygen present; consequently the candle goes out. The flame cannot exist when there is no oxygen. In this particular case, carbon in the candle combines with oxygen to give carbon dioxide.

Oxygen necessary to burn, and it's all used up	8
Air used up	7
No air, and necessary for burning	7
Oxygen all used up	7
Smothered	6
No air, not enough air	6
Not enough oxygen	6
Circulation interfered with, no draft, etc.	5
Because of the glass on top (no further explanation)	4
Hydrogen in jar	4
Air or oxygen in jar put it out	4
Jar cool or damp, so put it out	4
Various incorrect agents and relations. (Not enough hydrogen, smoke from candle, heat can't get out, etc.)	4
Wholly irrelevant and inadequate. (String under cover, something smells.)	2
Omitted	0
Don't know	0

RELIABILITY OF THE TEST

To determine the reliability of the test, both split-half and form-versus-form correlation coefficients were computed between the odd and even quantified scores on each form and between the total scores of individuals on the two forms. The results of the odd-even correlations are as follows: Form I (700 cases), .588, PE .017; Form II

(335 cases), .575, PE .025. The consistency of individuals in the level of their responses is found to be rather low. When the Spearman-Brown formula is applied, however, these correlations are stepped up to .740 for Form I and .730 for Form II. These coefficients are considerably higher than those found by Keen (23) for items of physical causality at any single age level.

Correlating the total scores of individuals on Form I of the test with the total scores of individuals on Form II, we obtain a coefficient of .534, PE .06 (65 cases). The Spearman-Brown formula is inapplicable as a correction for this coefficient, since the two forms of the test are not strictly comparable. The correlation between the two forms of the test is high in uncorrected form, however, when it is remembered that one form consisted of experiments involving strictly physical principles, the other a combination of items involving merely questions about phenomena in nature.

Age and Sex Trends in Quantified Scores

Age trends. — Since the quantified scores were derived by ratings based on the adequacy of the answer as an explanation of the phenomenon, it would be reasonable to expect an increase in the scores of individuals and groups with increasing age. It is a matter of common observation that older persons are more capable of giving adequate explanations (on the basis of prevailing scientific explanation) than are younger persons. If the answers given show a progression from low to high scores with increasing age, this would seem to be a partial validation of the method of questioning and obtaining the answers, and of the method of scoring. Unless the answers reflect the approximate level of ability of the subjects, this age progress would scarcely be found. Figures 1 and 2, in which the mean scores are plotted by age for the two sexes separately and for the total of the two sexes, show the mean quantified score by age for each question in the two forms of the test. The graphs in Figure 3, which give the mean quantified scores on Form I, Form II, and the two forms combined, show this age progress in summary.

An inspection of these graphs shows at once that on each question of the two forms, without exception, there is an increase in mean score with age. It will be noted that the increase with age is greater on some questions than on others. For instance, it is very slight on question 2 of Form I (penny in box), whereas it is marked on question 1 of Form II (What makes the wind blow?), and on question 7 of Form II (What makes the frost on the window panes?).

Fig. 1. — Mean Quantified Scores on Form I, According to Age and Sex

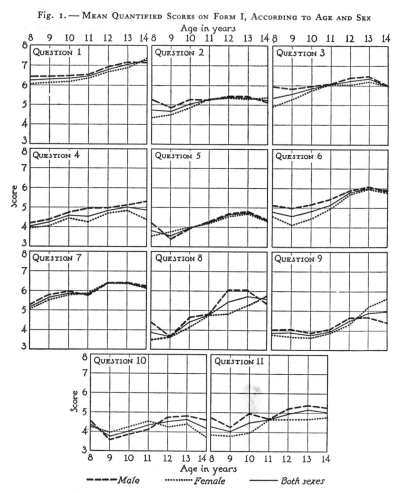

This difference is undoubtedly related to the difficulty of the question, and to the degree to which the questions may be affected by specific teaching. Whereas there is a consistent tendency for the answers to each question to improve with age, the improvement as measured is not consistent from age to age. The many irregularities in the several curves may be explained largely by the small number of cases in certain of the age groups. Although no means were calculated in age groups including fewer than 20 cases, the number was relatively small in the extreme age groups. There is a slight tendency for the mean score to drop at the 15–16-year level and for the mean score to be slightly higher at the 8-year level than at the 9-year. This may be accounted for, perhaps, by the selection of cases at these two extremes, as well as by the smaller sampling. As was pointed out in the description of subjects, only the more advanced 8-year-old children and the more retarded 15–16-year-old children are included in this study. Although, as will be shown later, there is very little relationship at age 12 between socio-economic status or the intelligence quotient and the quantified score, it seems possible

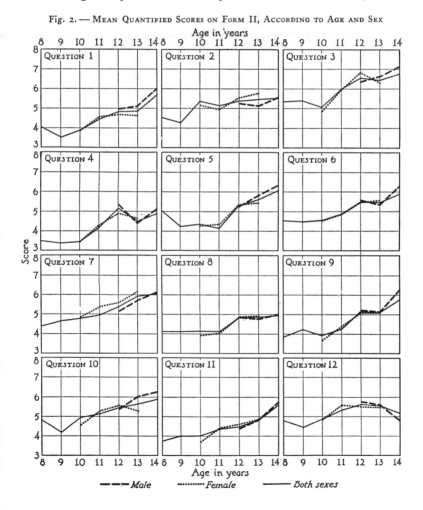

Fig. 2. — Mean Quantified Scores on Form II, According to Age and Sex

——— Male   ·········· Female   ——— Both sexes

Fig. 3. — MEAN QUANTIFIED SCORES ON FORM I, FORM II, AND THE TWO FORMS COMBINED, ACCORDING TO AGE AND SEX

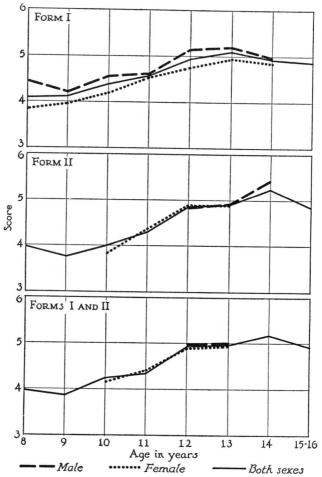

that this selection of cases may account for the superiority of the 8-year-old group and the inferiority of the 15–16-year-old group.

One tendency demonstrated is interesting in the light of Piaget's findings. Piaget has said that at approximately 12 years the child's explanation changes from a prelogical to a mechanical and logical explanation of causal phenomena. Although this quantitative analysis offers no clue to the logical structure of the child's answers, it is interesting to note that there is a greater rise in quantified score between the ages of 11 and 12 than between any other two consecutive ages.

Sex trends. — The quantified scores have been analyzed for each sex separately, because it was thought likely that there would be a sex difference in ability to answer questions involving causal relations. There is a rather widespread opinion that boys are more interested in the explanations of physical phenomena than are girls. Davis (6) has shown with young children that boys ask more questions relating to cause than do girls. This greater interest of boys in causal relations might well result in a greater knowledge of such relations, and consequently in a greater ability to explain the phenomena here in question. Figures 1, 2, and 3 present the mean quantified score according to age for the two sexes on each question of the two forms, and the mean scores per question for the two forms separately and combined. The data are complete for Form I, but for Form II the number of cases was not large enough at all levels to warrant the calculation of a mean score.

An inspection of the graphs shows quite clearly that the boys' answers are superior to those of the girls. This tendency is very marked and consistent in Form I of the test, the mean score on each question being higher for the boys than for the girls. Although on some questions there is crossing of the curves and girls are superior to boys at certain ages, on other questions boys are consistently superior to girls. On no question are girls consistently superior to boys.

For two reasons the data on Form II are less clear cut. One is their incompleteness, which precludes the possibility of drawing continuous curves over the entire age range for each sex. The other is that the difference between the two sexes is smaller, and consequently no consistent differences hold at the age ranges where the data are complete. Comparison of the partial curves with the curves for the two sexes combined shows that if the incomplete lines were extended on the basis of the relationship of one sex to the average for the two sexes, there would be much more crossing of the lines for the two sexes than was found in Form I. A comparison of the mean scores for children of all ages on each question shows small differences in mean score between the two sexes, and three questions on which the mean score is higher, though very slightly, for the girls than for the boys.

The items showing the greatest consistent superiority of boys over girls are Form I, question 4, block dropping; question 6, bulb on tube; and question 11, connected tubes. The questions upon which girls are superior to boys in total score, all ages combined, are Form II, question 2, "What makes the snow?"; question 7, "What makes the frost on the windows?"; and question 12, "How is it you can see yourself when you look into a mirror?"

It is interesting to note that the questions upon which the boys are definitely superior are all from Form I and are questions on which it is unlikely the child has had specific instruction, whereas the girls are slightly superior only on three questions from Form II that are very likely to have arisen in the child's experience and to have been answered by adults. This sex difference holds more or less for all the questions of Forms I and II. This might suggest that the superiority of boys over girls is more basic — that is, that whereas there is little sex difference on questions allowing for greater instruction and for greater experience with the phenomena, the boys are superior when confronted with novel phenomena requiring the application of general principles for explanation.

A sex difference in causal thinking has been found by Keen (23), who reports that boys receive significantly higher scores on the physical items of her test, whereas the difference is very slightly in favor of the girls on psychological items. Peterson (27) found boys slightly superior in ability to solve problems involving the general principle of the first-class lever, and Bedell (3) found boys superior to girls in ability to draw inferences from general science material. These results are in line with those of the present study.

Relationship of Quantified Scores to Socio-Economic Status, Intelligence, and School Grade

Relation to socio-economic status. — Zawerska (41) reports that children's causal explanations are rather closely linked with environment (residence in town or country) and with the immediate social environment. This seems quite possible. Socio-economic status has been found to be rather intimately related to the intelligence as well as to the education of adults. Offspring of parents of superior socio-economic status, superior intelligence, and superior education are likely to have advantages (more intelligent handling of questions, more facilities for study, more specific explanation or teaching, etc.) not available to children coming from lower socio-economic levels. With this possibility in mind, the quantified scores have been analyzed in relation to the socio-economic status of the child to determine whether the advantages which we know are related to high socio-economic status, and others which may be related, have operated to make the children in these upper groups more capable of giving adequate answers.

In the socio-economic analysis, a single age group (age 12) was used in order to prevent the age-score relationship from obscuring the socio-economic-score relation. Age 12 was chosen because of the relatively large number of cases in this group, and because the data on socio-economic status and intelligence were more complete for this age than for any other.

A picture of the relationship may be obtained by an inspection of the graphs in Figure 4, showing the mean quantified scores for each occupational group. The mean quantified score of the 12-year-old group on Form I, Form II, and the two forms combined was obtained for each occupational group. This mean score was divided by the number of items in the form to make the scores comparable from form to form.

It will be seen that there is no consistent tendency for children in higher socio-economic groups to receive higher quantified scores. Many of the groups, it is true, contain small numbers of cases, but the results are quite consistent in showing no relationship.

Relation to intelligence. — There is evidence in the literature that reasoning ability is closely correlated with intelligence. Burt (4) has found consistently high correlations. Winch (40) reports close correspondence between reasoning and age-grade placement, which he considers a measure of intelligence. Keen (23), however, found rather low correlations of intelligence with ability to give causal explanations. She concludes that intelligence is made up of many variables, of which reasoning, as she has measured it, is one.

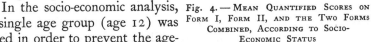

Fig. 4. — Mean Quantified Scores on Form I, Form II, and the Two Forms Combined, According to Socio-Economic Status

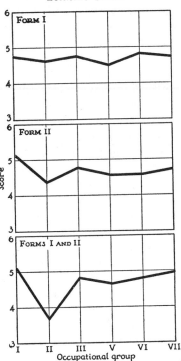

Correlation coefficients have been calculated between quantified scores and such intelligence test data as were available in the 12-year group. The correlation between Kuhlmann-Anderson IQ and quantified score total for Form I (45 cases) was .265, PE .091; for Form II (44 cases), .129, PE .100; and for the total of the two forms (44 cases), .182, PE .098. The correlation between Unit Aptitude quotients and quantified score total for Form I (73 cases) was .417, PE .065. The Unit Aptitude quotient is not, strictly speaking, an intelligence quotient, however, since aptitude is measured rather than intelligence as such. It might be expected, therefore, that the correlation of aptitude with quantified scores would be higher if training and experience affect reasoning ability as measured.

Relation to school grade. — Peterson (27), studying the ability of primary school children to generalize the principle of the lever, found that schooling was more closely related to this ability than was intelligence or chronological age, and concluded that schools seem to give a type of training which is general in its effect upon this specific ability. This finding is of interest as it bears upon the problem of the relation between maturation, or innate factors, and environment or experience as affecting causal thinking.

Since school grade gives a categorical rather than a continuous classification, the product-moment method of correlation is not strictly applicable, though it is the coefficient usually employed with similar data. Pearson coefficients were computed between school grade and quantified scores on the forms (using children aged 12) merely to see the trend of the relationship. The resulting coefficients were: grade and scores on Form I (145 cases), .405, PE .047; on Form II (66 cases), .390, PE .070; and on Forms I and II combined (65 cases), .445, PE .067. These figures suggested a positive relationship between score and schooling.

The mean score for children of a given age in every grade was then determined, and the resultant mean was divided by the number of items in the form to find the mean score per item. The findings for this group and for children aged 12 are shown in Figure 5. Because of the small number of cases in certain grades, not much reliance can be placed upon these means. There is, however, a fairly consistent tendency for the mean quantified score to increase with school grade, age being held constant. This may be due to the selected distribution of children in the grades, the more intelligent being in the higher grades, or it may be due to actual training, the children in higher grades having had more instruction along lines

Fig. 5. — Mean Quantified Scores at Age 12 and at All Ages on Form I, Form II,
and the Two Forms Combined, According to School Grade

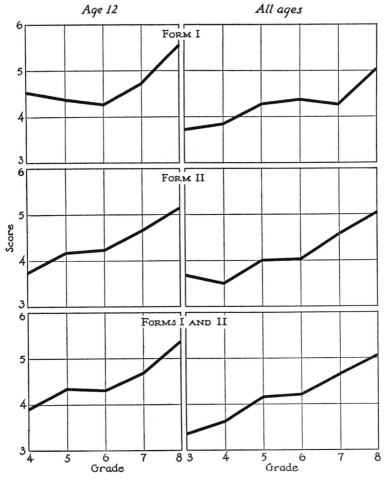

which might influence their answers. Figure 5 also shows the relationship between grade and mean quantified score per question when age is not held constant.

A comparison of the curves for quantified scores according to school grade and according to age shows a decided similarity between the two. For Form II, though not for Form I, there is a marked increase in score between grades 6 and 7, which corresponds to the increase between ages 11 and 12. The increase with grade is, however, more rapid thereafter than is the increase with age. The rapid rise after grade 6 might be explained by the fact that the majority of the seventh- and eighth-grade children were in a junior high school where general science is part of the curriculum. The phenomena in Form II are particularly likely to receive attention in such a course, a fact that may explain the difference between Forms I and II in the grade-score relationship.

SUMMARY

1. Answers given by the children were rated as to adequacy by 13 judges. Split-half reliability of the judgments approached unity. The rating values were converted into weighted scores, making comparable scores available for each answer to each question in the two forms.

2. The odd-even reliability coefficients of quantified scores were .588 for Form I and .575 for Form II. When the Spearman-Brown formula was applied, these were increased to .740 and .730, respectively. The correlation between scores on the two forms was .534.

3. The total score increases consistently with age. Since this is what would be expected, it is interpreted as a partial validation of the test as a measure of the child's concepts of causal relations.

4. The greatest increase between two ages is found between 11 and 12 years, the latter being the age at which Piaget fixes the appearance of mechanical and logical thinking. This is likewise the age, however, at which specific instruction in this kind of material (particularly the kind found in Form II) is being introduced into the school curriculum.

5. Boys were found to achieve higher scores than girls, particularly on Form I, where there is less chance for the influence of specific instruction and adult explanations to affect the results.

6. There is no consistent relationship between quantified scores and socio-economic status as measured by father's occupation. There is a very low correlation within a single age group between quantified scores and intelligence. There is a fairly high relationship between school grade and quantified scores, even within a single age group.

7. The higher relationship of quantified scores to school grade than to age, and the low relationship between quantified scores and intelligence and socio-economic status, suggest that training or experience, as acquired through the schools, outweighs intelligence or innate maturational factors in determining the ability of children to answer the questions included in this test.

IV. ANALYSIS OF NUMBER OF WORDS USED

Scoring Technique

The words used in each answer to each question were counted and recorded as a rough measure of language development. There is no direct evidence that the length of response is an adequate measure of language development. Certain evidence, however, points to the possibility of a relationship. McCarthy (25), Day (7), and Smith (36) have found that with preschool children the length of sentence is closely related to language development. LaBrant (24), in studying the use of subordinate clauses as a measure of language development, found an increase in length of subordinate clauses from nine years to adulthood. The brevity and incomplete sentence structure of the answers given in this investigation precluded the use of the subordinate clause as an index. The length of the answer was determined in order to find its relationship, if any, to age and to the quantified scores of the answers. The Mc-Carthy rules for scoring number of words (25, page 36) were adopted.

Consistency of the Measure

To determine the consistency of the number of words used as a measure, the split-half and form-versus-form correlations were found. Correlations were computed between number of words used in answering the odd and the even items of each form. On Form I (700 cases) the correlation is .717, PE .012; on Form II (335 cases), .721, PE .018. When these coefficients are stepped up by means of the Spearman-Brown formula, they are, respectively, .835 and .838. This indicates that there is a tendency for subjects to be consistently brief or expansive in answering the several questions; those using more words in their explanations of one item tend to use more in explaining other items also.

When the consistency from one form to another was determined, the correlation between total number of words used by individuals on Forms I and II (65 cases) was found to be .667, PE .046. It seems, therefore, that in using the number of words given in an explanation as a measure, we are using a measure that is reliable, that is, consistent for the individual from item to item and from form to form.

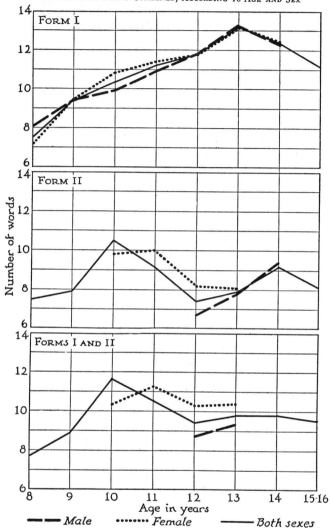

Fig. 6. — MEAN NUMBER OF WORDS PER QUESTIONS ON FORM I, FORM II, AND THE TWO FORMS COMBINED, ACCORDING TO AGE AND SEX

FORM I

FORM II

FORMS I AND II

Number of words

Age in years

– – Male •••••• Female —— Both sexes

Relationship of Number of Words Used to Age and Sex

Age trends. — The relation between age and number of words used in an answer was determined. Figure 6 shows the findings for the two sexes combined, presenting the mean number of words per answer to questions on Forms I and II separately and on the two forms combined.

There is a consistent and definite increase with age, except at 14 years, in the number of words used in the answers to questions of Form I. Although the data are not complete for all ages of Form II, this tendency does not seem to hold true on this form. The means for the individual questions as well as for Form II as a whole show that there is a peak in the number of words used at about 10 years of age, preceded and followed by a definitely smaller mean number of words. A similar relationship is found for Forms I and II combined, though it is due entirely to the data on Form II.

The only plausible explanation of the discrepancy between the curves for Forms I and II is that the nature of the questions is again operating to produce a difference. The questions on Form II, as has previously been pointed out, deal with more general phenomena of nature, which are more closely tied up with the experience of the child. The child may have developed a ready answer, either independently or by instruction. He may have had previous occasion to formulate the answers in words. The questions on Form I, on the other hand, deal with phenomena with which the child is less likely to have had experience, at least in the form in which they are presented in these experiments. He has never had occasion to formulate an answer to these questions and may, therefore, use more words in trying to explain a relationship than would be necessary if he had previously thought it out clearly.

The possibility that the quality of the answers as determined by the quantified scores might be related to the number of words used will be discussed later.

Sex differences in number of words. — All studies which compare the two sexes with respect to language report a tendency for girls to exceed boys in the quantity of language used. McCarthy (25) and Day (7), using preschool children as subjects, have found that girls consistently exceed boys in length of sentence. LaBrant (24), analyzing the compositions of school age children, found no sex difference with respect to the use of subordinate clauses but found a definite superiority on the part of girls in the length of compositions. In her fourth- to ninth-grade groups, boys wrote only 86 per cent as much as girls, and in her group of 16-year-olds only 83 per cent as much. She offers two possible explanations of this discrepancy on the basis of training: (1) that girls are trained to conform to school requirements more readily, and write longer papers because they are more generally approved and (2) girls find handwriting less difficult than do boys, and thus produce more composition in a given period.

Figure 6 shows the relationship found in this study between the number of words used by the two sexes. These graphs present the mean number of words used at each age by both sexes on Forms I and II separately and on the two forms combined. From them we see that there is no clear-cut sex difference in the number of words used. The curves cross, indicating that from age to age there is no consistent tendency for one sex to be superior. A comparison of the mean number of words used in answering each question, all ages combined, shows that girls used more than boys on six questions from Form I, boys more than girls on five questions, though all the differences are very small; on Form II girls used more words than boys on nine questions, boys more than girls on three, though again all the differences are very small. For all questions and all ages the mean number of words on Form I is 11.24 for boys, 11.09 for girls; on Form II, 8.09 for boys, 8.68 for girls. On Forms I and II combined, the mean number of words for boys is 9.38, for girls 10.25. These differences are negligible, although in the expected direction.

There is no clear-cut explanation for the absence of the expected sex difference in number of words. There is, however, as will be shown, a relationship between the quantified score and the number of words used. This seems to indicate that language development is not the one factor determining the length of response, but that ability to answer has also operated to affect the length of response.

RELATIONSHIP OF NUMBER OF WORDS USED TO SOCIO-ECONOMIC STATUS, INTELLIGENCE, AND SCHOOL GRADE

The relationship between the number of words a child uses to express his answer and such factors as socio-economic status, intelligence, and school grade is also of interest, as much from the standpoint of language development as from any other.

Socio-economic status and number of words. — As in the analysis of the relationship between socio-economic status and quantified scores, a single age group (age 12) has been used in order to eliminate the relationship between age and language which might obscure the relationship between socio-economic status and language. Again, for the same reasons as before, the correlational method is not entirely applicable. The only method for determining the relationship between these two variables which is applicable to the data is a comparison of the mean number of words used per question by members of the several socio-economic groups. These means were determined for each form and for the two forms combined. Figure 7 shows the data for Form I; the number of persons in any one socio-economic group who took Form II is too small to supply meaningful data. It will be noted that on Form I there is a tendency for the number of words used to decrease with decreasing socio-economic status, although this tendency is very slight.

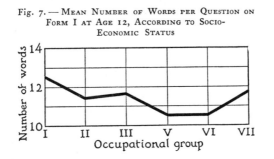

Fig. 7. — MEAN NUMBER OF WORDS PER QUESTION ON FORM I AT AGE 12, ACCORDING TO SOCIO-ECONOMIC STATUS

Intelligence and number of words. — Correlations were calculated between number of words used and intelligence quotients (age 12 only). The correlation between number of words on Form I and Kuhlmann-Anderson IQ (43 cases) was .358, PE .09; between words used in Form II and Kuhlmann-Anderson IQ (44 cases), .337, PE .09; and between words in Forms I and II combined and Kuhlmann-Anderson IQ (44 cases), .425, PE .083. The correlation between Unit Aptitude quotient and words used on Form I (73 cases) was .342, PE .07; and between Unit Aptitude Mental Age and words used in Form I (73 cases), .253, PE .07. It will be noted that the number of words used bears a higher relation to intelligence than does the quantified score on the answers.

McCarthy (25), in studying preschool children, finds that the curve for mean length of sentence in relation to mental age is the same as the curve for mean length of sentence in relation to chronological age. Here, however, it was found that length of response is related to intelligence when age is held constant. Our measure is not comparable to McCarthy's because factors other than language ability are probably affecting the length of response.

School grade and number of words. — Here again the correlational method is not applicable, although it is the usual method of treating this kind of data. A more applicable technique for showing the relationship between school grade and number of words used is that of determining the mean number of words used per question by children aged 12 in each school grade. The data for Form I are shown in Figure 8. From this graph we see that when age is held constant, there is a definite tendency for the number of words used to increase with the school grade. For Form II the number of cases in one group is in many instances so small that the means are wholly unreliable, but the tendency is in the direction expected.

The relation between grade and total scores on the form when age is not held constant was also determined. (See Figure 8.) For both forms there was found to be a definite increase in number of words with advance in school grade, though the findings are again less consistent for Form II, for the same reason as before.

RELATION BETWEEN QUANTIFIED SCORES AND NUMBER OF WORDS USED

Correlation coefficients were computed between the total quantified score on each form of the test and the total number of words used in answering that form of the test. A similar coefficient was

Fig. 8. — MEAN NUMBER OF WORDS PER QUESTION ON FORM I AT AGE 12 AND AT ALL AGES, ACCORDING TO SCHOOL GRADE

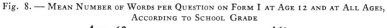
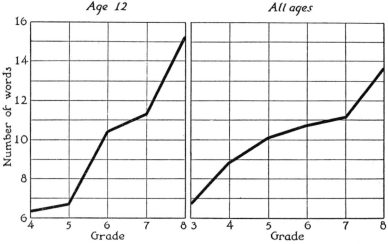

TABLE 9. — CORRELATION BETWEEN TOTAL SCORES AND
TOTAL NUMBER OF WORDS USED

Form	Number of Cases	Correlation	Probable Error
Form I	145	.486	.043
Form II	66	.482	.064
Forms I and II . .	65	.452	.066

found with the two forms combined. (See Table 9.) It is fairly evident that there is a definite relationship between the number of words used in answering the questions and the quality of the answers as measured by the quantified scores.

Figure 9 presents the relation between the mean number of words used by all subjects at each age on Form I of the test and the mean quantified scores of the same groups on that form. An inspection of this graph shows that, allowing for different proportions, the two curves are fairly similar.

It is difficult to determine from these data the causal relationship between length and quality of answers. There are two possible explanations. The first is that in evaluating the answers the raters were unduly influenced by the length of the response. Since the typical group answers which were rated were not necessarily made up of individual answers of the same length, there was no way for

Fig. 9. — COMPARISON BETWEEN MEAN NUMBER OF WORDS PER QUESTION
AND MEAN QUANTIFIED SCORES ON FORM I, ACCORDING TO AGE

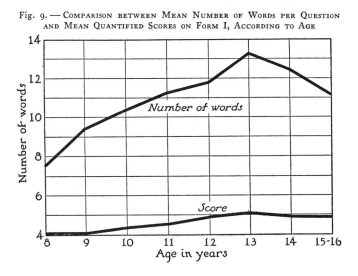

the raters to know of the individual differences in length of response. It is possible, however, that the score assigned to a typical answer was affected by the length of the answer, in that the more complete, and therefore longer, answer gave a more adequate basis for classification. When the answer consisted of a very few words, it became a matter of judgment as to just how much more was implied. It is possible that the longer and more complete the answer, the higher the rating, because it could be based upon concrete evidence rather than unverbalized implications. A second possibility is that the child who best understood the phenomenon in question was best able to express this explanation in words — to give a more complete answer. It is very probable that the two explanations combined to produce the relationship between the quantified score and the number of words used.

SUMMARY

1. The number of words used in answering individual questions has been shown to be relatively consistent for the same subject. This consistency is found also between the totals on the two forms.

2. The number of words used in the answers increases consistently with age on Form I of the test, although the increase is not consistent on Form II. This lack of consistent increase on Form II may perhaps be due to the nature of the items.

3. There are no consistent sex differences in the number of words used. There are sex differences on some specific questions, but not between totals on the two forms. The fact that there is a relationship between quantified scores and number of words used, and that boys receive higher quantified scores consistently, may offset the tendency, which has generally been found, for girls to use more words than boys in language situations.

4. There is but a slight relationship between socio-economic status and the number of words used in the explanations; there is some correlation (about .35) between number of words and intelligence; and a slight relationship, when age is held constant, between school grade and number of words.

5. There is a definite relationship (.48) between quantified scores and the number of words used in the explanations, for which there are two probable explanations: that the scoring of the answers has been influenced by the number of words used, and that the child who actually understands the explanation best gives a more complete, and therefore longer, explanation.

V. RATINGS USING PIAGET'S CLASSIFICATIONS

METHOD USED IN EVALUATION OF RATINGS

The author attempted to classify each answer to each question according to the classification of Piaget (30), which includes seventeen types of causal thought. It soon became obvious that the task was too difficult and too much a matter of judgment to be left to one person. The cooperation of two other persons was therefore enlisted. Two professors in the Institute of Child Welfare, both directly concerned with this research and both interested in and familiar with Piaget's work, worked with the author in the classification of the answers. Three entirely independent classifications of each answer were thus obtained.

Piaget's explanations of his seventeen types of thought were soon found to be quite inadequate for an understanding of their nature. The best definitions that could be found in his discussion were abstracted, however, together with examples when these were given. Each rater was provided with a set of these definitions and examples, and a copy of all the typical answers to each question on the two forms. The types of causal thought, with their definitions and examples, were as follows:

PIAGET'S SEVENTEEN TYPES OF CAUSAL RELATION
IN CHILD THOUGHT

1. *Motivational causality.*—A psychological motive is the cause of things. God or men send us dreams because we have done things which we ought not to have done. Things are conscious, or specially made by man.

2. *Finalism.* — Simple finality without origins or consequences of finalism being noticed. River flows so as to go into the lake. Not necessary for river to be conscious or have a motive.

3. *Phenomenistic causality.* — Two facts given together in perception, and such that no relation subsists between them except that of contiguity in time and space. Pebble sinks to bottom of water because it is white. No concept of relations.

4. *Participation.* — Two things with some resemblance or affinity can act upon each other at a distance. One a source of emanations, the other an emanation from the first. Shadows in room emanate from shadows out-of-doors.

5. *Magical causality.* — Gestures, thoughts, etc., charged with efficacy. Certain word acts on certain thing. White pebble makes water lilies grow.

6. *Moral causality.* — Moral necessity. Boats have to float, otherwise they would be no use.

7. *Artificialistic causality.* — Event explained by intention or motive at back of it, but child doesn't ask himself how this intention worked itself out in action. Event or object to be explained is conceived as the object of human creative activity.

8. *Animistic causality.* — An internal biological tendency that is both alive and conscious. Clouds move because they are alive.

9. *Dynamic causality.* — Animism gone, but still sees in objects forces that are capable of explaining their activity and movements.

10. *Reaction of surrounding medium.* — No animism. Continuity and contact. Clouds driven along by the air which they produce in their flight.

11. *Mechanical causality.* — Explanation by contact and transference of movement. No internal force at all. Wind pushes the clouds. Pedals make bicycle go.

12. *Causality by generation.* — Things are born out of each other. Clouds come out of smoke, air, fire. Sun comes out of fiery cloud.

13. *Substantial identification.* — Bodies are born from each other, but are not endowed with power of growth. Sun is a collection of clouds rolled up into a ball.

14. *Schemas of condensation and rarefaction.* — Used to explain qualitative differences in substances. Hardness of stone comes from the fact that earth is close; water light because it is thin, liquid; wood heavy because big, thick, full, etc.

15. *Atomistic composition.* — Substances made up of particles tightly or loosely packed together. Stone is made of little stones, which are made of grains of earth.

16. *Spatial explanation.* — Explains rise of water level when pebble is put into water by volume of immersed body. Explains shadows by perspective.

17. *Explanation by logical deduction.* — Explanation by the principle of sufficient reason. Water flows into the second of the connected tubes because water can go equally well in both directions. Uses concepts of density, specific weight, etc.

There was considerable disagreement among the raters. Since in a few instances not all three raters made a judgment of a question, the results were tabulated separately where there are three judgments, two judgments, and one judgment, respectively, on an answer. Where three individuals rated the questions (510 cases) it was found that all three agreed on 108, or 21.76 per cent, of the items; two raters agreed on 245, or 48.04 per cent, of the items; and none of the raters agreed on 157, or 30.76 per cent, of the items. Where there were only two ratings (37 cases), it was found that the two raters agreed on 19, or 51.35 per cent, of the items, and disagreed on 18, or 48.65 per cent, of the items.

It was noted that the agreement was higher, in general, in the classification of the answers on Form II than on Form I. This may be explained in part by the fact that the questions used in Form II more closely approximate the kind of material used by Piaget, upon which the classification into types of causal thought was originally based.

The raters reported a great deal of difficulty in the classification of answers according to this schema. There were three types of difficulty. One was in the correct interpretation of the categories, that is, in maintaining a clear and distinct differentiation between different types of explanations. A second difficulty was finding a category into which each of the answers would fit logically. It was found that a number of the types of causality as outlined by Piaget were not represented in this data, and that many of the answers which were obtained in this study did not seem to fit into his schema of classification. The third difficulty was in interpreting what the child meant by his answer. It is obvious that the child has not expressed himself completely in these brief responses. It was nearly impossible to decide whether many answers implied prelogical types of thought which were not actually expressed, or whether other answers couched in prelogical language should be interpreted as representing the child's true mode of thinking. It was decided to base the classification of answers as nearly as possible upon their face value, since that was the only constant basis for judgment.

The extent of the disagreement between raters in the classification of answers according to Piaget's types suggests three criticisms of his schema of classification: (1) His classification of causal thought into seventeen types is inadequate — that is, that the answers given by a large sample of children do not fall naturally into these seventeen types. (2) Certain of the types of causality are very specific to a certain kind of question, and do not deserve a special category. For instance, no answers were found which could be classified as type 14 — schemas of condensation and rarefaction. On the other hand, type 11, mechanical causality, includes such a large proportion of the cases that it is too inclusive. (3) The fact that there is such a wide disagreement between three trained raters in the classification of the answers suggests that the matter of individual judgment enters to a large extent into the classification. It is impossible to put a great deal of reliance upon such a classification, particularly when it is based upon the judgment of one person.

In spite of the initial disagreement in classification, it was felt that a workable and useful classification on the basis of Piaget was possible. A conference of the three raters was therefore held, at which an attempt was made to reconcile the differences in judgment and to arrive at the best classification for each answer. Many of the differences disappeared upon reconsideration of the data. Misunderstandings of the definitions were cleared up; different interpretations of the answers were reconciled. In most instances it was possible to reach agreement as to the classification of the answers. Where agreement of all three raters could not be reached, the opinion of the majority was accepted. The result was a complete classification of all the answers into Piaget's seventeen types of causal thought and one new category, type 18, called "trickery," in which the child implies that there is some trick in the experiment — that what he sees is not the whole story. The frequency in this category is very small.

The Piaget type into which each of the typical answers to the question "Why does the candle go out?" was classified is given below. The numbers are those used to identify the types. (See pages 51 and 52.)

Oxygen necessary to burn, and it's all used up	17
Air used up	17
No air, and necessary for burning	17
Oxygen all used up	17
No air, not enough air	17
Not enough oxygen	17
Hydrogen in jar	11
Circulation interfered with, no draft, etc.	11
Smothered	9
Air or oxygen in jar put it out	9
Because of the glass on top (no further explanation)	3
Wholly irrelevant and inadequate. (String under cover, something smells.)	3
Jar cool or damp, so put it out	3
Various incorrect agents and relations. (Not enough hydrogen, smoke from candle, heat can't get out, etc.)	3
Omitted	0
Don't know	0

ANALYSIS BY QUESTION AND FORM

A great variation was noted from question to question in the percentage of answers falling into each type of causal thinking. Logical deduction comprises 83.1 per cent of the answers given to question 1 of Form I, but only 2.5 per cent of the answers given to question 2 of Form I. There were similar differences on most classifications. This is probably to b⌐ explained in terms of the nature and difficulty of the question.

Table 10 presents the percentage of all answers on Form I, Form II, and the two forms combined which were classified within each Piaget type of causality.

It will be noted that none of the answers given were classified under the following types: participation; artificialistic causality; reaction of surrounding medium; schemas of condensation and rarefaction; and atomistic composition. In the opinion of the raters, there were no answers representing these types of thought. This might be attributed to the age of the children studied in this investigation, but such an explanation seems unlikely because all these types are of a higher level (according to Piaget) than many of

TABLE 10. — PERCENTAGE OF ALL ANSWERS FALLING INTO EACH OF PIAGET'S CLASSIFICATIONS

Type of Causality	Form I	Form II	Forms I and II
1. Motivational	0.1	1.1	0.3
2. Finalistic.	0.4	0.5	0.3
3. Phenomenistic.	21.8	18.9	20.8
4. Participative	0.0	0.0	0.0
5. Magical	0.2	2.9	1.1
6. Moral	0.8	1.0	0.9
7. Artificialistic	0.0	0.0	0.0
8. Animistic.	0.3	0.2	0.3
9. Dynamic	8.7	1.7	6.3
10. Surrounding medium.	0.0	0.0	0.0
11. Mechanical	37.7	41.4	38.9
12. Generative	0.0	1.4	0.4
13. Substantial identification	0.0	0.2	0.1
14. Condensation, rarefaction.	0.0	0.0	0.0
15. Atomistic.	0.0	0.0	0.0
16. Spatial	0.1	0.0	0.1
17. Logical.	22.7	24.7	23.4
18. Trickery*	0.2	0.2	0.2
Unclassifiable	7.1	5.9	6.7

* Classification added by the present investigator.

the types for which there is a fair percentage of answers. Two of the types which were not represented (14 and 15) Piaget places at a relatively high stage of logical development. The absence of answers of these types is undoubtedly explained by the kind of questions used in this investigation. Schemas of condensation and rarefaction, and atomistic composition, are both narrow classifications, applicable to a very few kinds of questions, which, as it happens, are not found in this investigation. It is the opinion of the author that these types are unnecessary subdivisions of larger and more useful categories.

An inspection of Table 10 shows that the following types of causal thought are found in very low frequency: motivational type, averaging 0.3 per cent on both forms and found on but three of the questions asked; finalism, averaging 0.3 per cent on both forms, found on but five questions; magical causality, averaging 1.1 per cent, found on twelve questions; moral causality, averaging 0.9 per cent, found on three questions; animistic causality, averaging 0.3 per cent, found on four questions; causality by generation, 0.4 per cent, found on only one question; substantial identification, 0.1 per cent, found on one question; spatial explanation, averaging 0.1 per cent, found on one question; and trickery, averaging 0.2 per cent, found on three questions.

This leaves but five types of causal thought that are represented by fairly high percentages. These include: phenomenistic causality, 20.8 per cent, found on all questions; dynamic causality, 6.3 per cent, found on nine questions; mechanical causality, 38.9 per cent, found on all questions; logical deduction, 23.4 per cent, found on all questions; and answers that cannot be classified (omitted, incomplete, incomprehensible, "don't know"), 6.7 per cent, found on all but one question.

These results check well with the results of Huang (19), Johnson and Josey (22), and Keen (23), who find that many of the prelogical types of causal explanation occur in low frequency. Huang and Johnson and Josey included younger children in their experiments; Keen used children from the sixth grade up. All agree that magical, moralistic, finalistic, and animistic answers are very rarely found.

There are some rather interesting differences between the two forms as to the types of answers given. On the whole, the answers given in Form II are superior, on the basis of Piaget's age analysis for the different types, to the answers given in Form I. Figure 10,

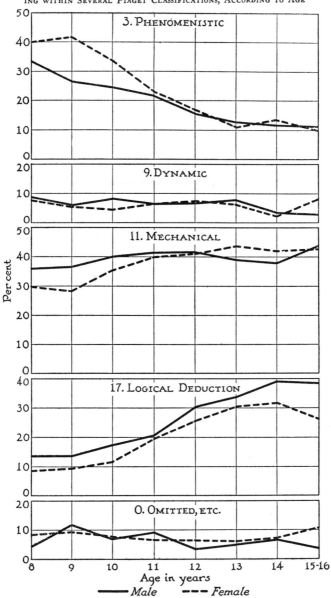

which presents the age curves by form for the five most frequent types, shows some of these differences. There are slightly more phenomenistic answers on Form I than on Form II, and definitely more dynamic answers. The percentage of mechanical answers is higher on the second form throughout the age range, but the logical deduction type, though more frequent on Form II at the later ages, is more frequent on Form I at the earlier ages.

Similarly, from Table 10 it will be seen that there are more answers of the motivational type on Form II; slightly more magical answers on Form II; and that there are no answers classified as causality by generation or substantial identification in Form I.

The presence of more dynamic answers, fewer mechanical answers, and slightly fewer answers involving logical deduction on Form I can perhaps be explained by the fact that the questions in this form are more novel — less subject to actual instruction — than those on Form II. There is, however, much evidence that instruction accounts for prelogical answers on Form II. For instance, there are many answers which involve fairy tales ("Giants' snoring causes thunder," "Rainbow is star's clothing hung out to dry," "Rainbow is God's sign that there will be no more rain").

AGE, SEX, AND SOCIO-ECONOMIC TRENDS

Age changes. — Table 11 presents the percentage, at each age, of the total answers on Forms I and II which is made up of each type of causal thinking. Figure 10 shows the age trends more clearly.

The most striking changes with age in the percentage of each type of causal thinking are found in the phenomenistic, mechanical, and logical deduction categories. Phenomenistic answers comprise 37.3 per cent of the answers at age 8, whereas at age 15–16 they comprise but 10.3 per cent. The decline is fairly consistent from age to age. There is an increase in the percentage of answers of the mechanical type from 32.5 per cent at 8 years to 42.9 per cent at 15–16 years. A striking increase is found in the logical deduction type, from 10.7 per cent at 8 years to 31.6 per cent at 15–16 years, with a peak at 14, when the percentage is 35.6 per cent. It may be noted, in passing, that each of these types of causality belongs in the materialistic category which will be discussed later.

Very little age change is noted in other types of causal thinking. The percentage of unclassifiable answers remains quite constant. The dynamic causality type is found slightly less frequently at the

TABLE 11. — PERCENTAGE OF ALL ANSWERS FALLING INTO SEVERAL PIAGET
CLASSIFICATIONS, ACCORDING TO AGE

Type of Causality	Age in Years								
	8	9	10	11	12	13	14	15–16	All Ages
1. Motivational . . .	0.3	0.5	0.3	0.5	0.4	0.4	0.3	0.4	0.3
2. Finalistic	0.0	0.5	0.7	0.5	0.3	0.3	0.4	0.2	0.3
3. Phenomenistic. . .	37.3	32.5	29.5	22.4	16.1	11.9	12.4	10.3	20.8
5. Magical	1.6	2.6	1.3	1.0	1.0	0.5	0.3	0.2	1.1
6. Moral	1.2	0.5	1.4	0.9	0.6	0.8	1.1	1.0	0.9
8. Animistic.	0.6	0.2	0.6	0.3	0.3	0.2	0.0	0.0	0.3
9. Dynamic	8.3	5.8	6.3	6.2	7.1	6.7	2.9	5.7	6.3
11. Mechanical	32.5	33.2	37.4	40.5	41.1	41.0	39.5	42.9	38.9
12. Generative	0.3	0.8	0.8	0.2	0.5	0.3	0.3	0.2	0.4
13. Substantial identification	0.0	0.0	0.0	0.0	0.0	0.2	0.3	0.0	0.1
16. Spatial	0.0	0.0	0.0	0.1	0.0	0.2	0.1	0.0	0.1
17. Logical.	10.7	11.8	14.1	19.8	28.1	32.0	35.6	31.6	23.4
18. Trickery*	0.6	0.7	0.5	0.0	0.0	0.1	0.0	0.1	0.2

*Classification added by the present investigator.

upper ages, but the change is very small. Animistic causality is found in a frequency of but a fraction of one per cent up through age 13, with none thereafter. Motivation type is found in fractions of one per cent throughout the age range; finalism in fractions of one per cent at all but the 8-year level. Magical answers decrease slightly with age, from 2.6 per cent at age 9, which is the peak, to 0.2 at age 15–16. Moral causality is found in a frequency of nearly one per cent throughout the range. Causality by generation shows no age trend, but a fractional percentage is found throughout. Substantial identification is found only in ages 12–14, in very small percentages of the total. Spatial relation explanations are found in small fractions of one per cent at ages 11, 13, and 14. Trickery is found scattered in fractional percentages over the range.

It is evident that for the types of causality most rarely found there is no apparent age relationship, while for the most frequent types there is definite age relationship; phenomenistic explanations are replaced by mechanical explanations or logical deduction, and mechanical explanations are replaced by the logical deduction type.

Sex differences in causal types. — Table 12 presents according to sex the percentage of answers of each type. The sex distribution for the types of causality having the highest frequency is shown graphically in Figure 11.

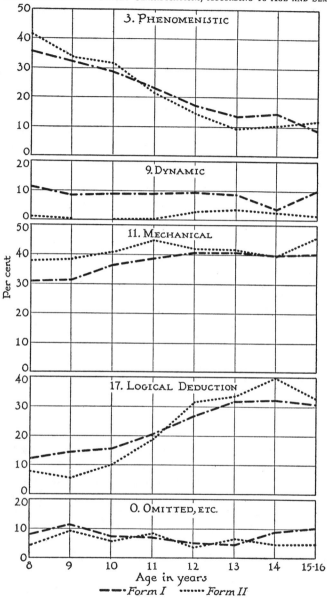

Fig. 11. — PERCENTAGE OF ALL ANSWERS ON FORM I AND ON FORM II FALLING WITHIN SEVERAL PIAGET CLASSIFICATIONS, ACCORDING TO AGE AND SEX

3. PHENOMENISTIC

9. DYNAMIC

11. MECHANICAL

17. LOGICAL DEDUCTION

0. OMITTED, ETC.

Per cent

Age in years

——·Form I ········Form II

TABLE 12. — PERCENTAGE OF ALL ANSWERS FALLING INTO SEVERAL PIAGET CLASSIFICATIONS, ACCORDING TO SEX

Type of Causality	Form I		Form II		Forms I and II	
	Boys	Girls	Boys	Girls	Boys	Girls
1. Motivational . . .	0.1	0.0	0.9	1.3	0.3	0.5
2. Finalistic.	0.2	0.5	0.4	0.5	0.3	0.5
3. Phenomenistic. . .	19.3	24.4	17.6	20.1	18.8	22.9
5. Magical	0.1	0.3	2.8	3.0	0.9	1.2
6. Moral	0.4	1.2	1.0	1.0	0.6	1.2
8. Animistic.	0.2	0.4	0.2	0.1	0.2	0.3
9. Dynamic	8.9	8.5	1.6	1.8	6.5	6.1
11. Mechanical	38.9	36.3	40.7	42.2	39.5	38.4
12. Generative	0.0	0.0	1.3	1.4	0.4	0.5
13. Substantial identification	0.0	0.0	0.2	0.3	0.1	0.1
16. Spatial	0.1	0.1	0.0	0.0	0.1	0.1
17. Logical.	25.4	19.9	27.8	22.2	26.0	20.8
18. Trickery*	0.1	0.4	0.2	0.3	0.1	0.3
Unclassifiable . . .	6.4	7.8	6.0	5.9	6.2	7.1

*Classification added by the present investigator.

The greatest sex differences are again found in the most frequent types of answer. On each form it was found that girls give a higher percentage of phenomenistic answers than do boys, the difference being fairly consistent throughout the age range. Boys give on the whole slightly more mechanical answers than do girls, although on Form II the girls give a higher percentage, and there is some inconsistency. Boys give more mechanical answers at the earlier ages, girls slightly more at the later ages. Boys consistently give a higher percentage of answers of the logical deduction type than do girls. The difference is fairly large on both forms at most ages. There is no apparent sex difference in the percentage of answers of the dynamic type, nor of unclassifiable answers, the two remaining types which have fairly large percentages. Girls give very slightly more of the following types, though the total frequency on most of these items is very small and the differences are but fractions of one per cent: finalism, magical causality, moral causality, and trickery.

The greater number of girls giving phenomenistic answers, and of boys giving mechanical and logical deduction answers, agrees well with the superiority of boys over girls in quantified scores, since the latter two types have far higher score values than the former.

Socio-economic differences in causal types. — Table 13 presents the distribution of the several types according to the socio-economic

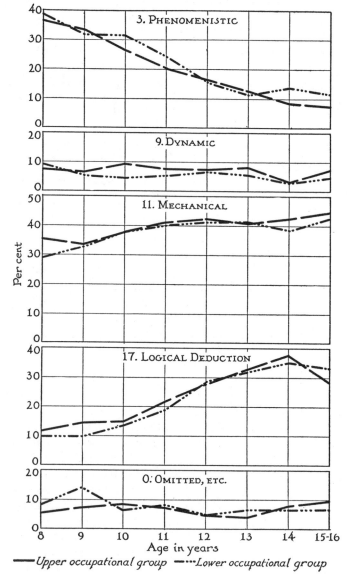

status of the children, and Figure 12 gives the same data in graphic form. It will be seen that the differences between the three upper economic groups (I, II, and III) and the three lower economic groups (V, VI, and VII) are small. Less difference is found than was found between sexes. Children in the lower economic groups give a slightly higher percentage of phenomenistic answers; those in the upper economic groups give only very slightly more mechanical answers. There is no difference between the two groups in logical deduction. The upper group appeals slightly more frequently to dynamic causes. As for those types which are found in smaller frequencies, the lower groups give slightly more magical answers, but the other differences are not greater than a few tenths of one per cent. It may be concluded that type of causal thinking is not related to the socio-economic level of the child.

TABLE 13. — PERCENTAGE OF ALL ANSWERS FALLING INTO SEVERAL PIAGET CLASSIFICATIONS, ACCORDING TO OCCUPATIONAL GROUPINGS

Type of Causality	Form I		Form II		Forms I and II	
	Upper Occupational Group	Lower Occupational Group	Upper Occupational Group	Lower Occupational Group	Upper Occupational Group	Lower Occupational Group
1. Motivational . . .	0.1	0.1	1.1	1.1	0.2	0.5
2. Finalistic	0.3	0.4	0.3	0.5	0.3	0.5
3. Phenomenistic. . .	21.5	22.1	18.5	19.1	20.8	20.8
5. Magical	0.2	0.2	2.4	3.0	0.7	1.4
6. Moral	0.9	0.7	1.1	1.0	0.9	0.8
8. Animistic.	0.3	0.4	0.1	0.2	0.2	0.3
9. Dynamic	9.3	8.1	1.3	1.8	7.6	5.5
11. Mechanical . . . ʼ.	38.3	37.1	43.7	40.6	39.4	38.5
12. Generative	0.0	0.0	1.1	1.5	0.2	0.6
13. Substantial identification	0.0	0.0	0.2	0.2	0.0	0.1
16. Spatial	0.1	0.1	0.0	0.0	0.0	0.1
17. Logical.	22.5	23.0	25.6	24.3	23.2	23.5
18. Trickery*	0.3	0.1	0.2	0.2	0.3	0.1
Unclassifiable . . .	6.3	7.8	4.7	6.4	6.0	7.2

*Classification added by the present investigator.

SUMMARY AND INTERPRETATION OF FINDINGS

1. Each answer to the questions was classified into one of Piaget's types of causal thinking by a concensus of the opinions of three qualified judges. Analysis was then made of these types.

2. Piaget's classification of causal thinking into seventeen types is criticized on three scores: (1) that the answers actually given do not fit naturally into these types; (2) that the types are of unequal value, some being too inclusive, some so specific as not to be represented at all by these data; and (3) that personal judgment enters to a great extent into the classification. Three trained raters disagreed considerably in independent ratings based upon these categories.

3. Only four types of causal thinking were found in large enough frequencies to allow for analysis of age relationships. Phenomenistic causality declined with age; mechanical explanation and logical deduction increased in frequency with age; dynamism showed no age relationship.

4. Girls gave slightly more answers of the phenomenistic type, boys slightly more of the mechanical and logical deduction types. This finding checks with the superiority of boys on the quantified scores. Socio-economic differences were very slight but were in the expected direction.

5. There was great overlapping between age groups in the types of answers found. Finalistic, magical, moralistic, and dynamic answers are found even at the 15–16-year level, though Piaget (30) calls these prelogical types, to be found in the earlier years only. Mechanical and logical answers are found with a fair frequency at 8 years of age. Every type of answer found in large enough frequency to eliminate chance factors is found over the entire age range. This suggests that causality does not develop in definite stages, with types of response characteristic of one age and not another. At least, it does not so develop at the ages under consideration in this study.

6. On different questions we find different proportions in the several types of response. Some questions elicit high percentages of mechanical and logical answers, others low percentages. Some elicit more dynamic, some more magical answers, etc., which suggests that the type of response is dependent in part upon the question involved; that specificity rather than a general level is characteristic of the child's causal thinking; and that the level of response is determined more by the nature of the question than by the age of the child.

VI. SEQUENCE AND MATERIALISTIC CLASSIFICATIONS

METHOD AND PURPOSE OF SEQUENCE CLASSIFICATION

Upon analyzing Piaget's seventeen types of causal thinking, it became apparent that the types fell into more or less definite sequences. Instead of dividing the types into logical and prelogical as Piaget did, the author divided them upon the basis of the type of agent involved in the explanation. It was found that there were certain types of explanations which involved a materialistic cause — that is, in which the only cause was some reaction of a material substance. In another group the principal cause as given was nonmaterialistic — that is, some person, some spirit, some force was called upon to explain the materialistic change. In this nonmaterialistic sequence two subdivisions were immediately apparent. Certain types of answers postulated a force within the material substance (as in dynamic causality), or a personality, an individual (as in animistic causality). Certain other types postulated a force or person outside of the material substance involved, which acted from the outside upon this substance (as in magical explanations, i. e., "God makes the rainbow").

Consequently, each of the seventeen Piaget types and our new type, "trickery," were classified into the proper sequence. The classification as finally adopted was as follows:

1. Materialistic Sequence
   - 3. Phenomenistic causality
   - 10. Reaction of surrounding medium
   - 11. Mechanical causality
   - 14. Schemas of condensation and rarefaction
   - 15. Atomistic composition
   - 16. Spatial explanation
   - 17. Logical deduction
   - 18. Trickery

2. Nonmaterialistic Sequence
   - a. External
     - 1. Motivational
     - 2. Finalism
     - 5. Magical causality
     - 6. Moral causality
     - 7. Artificialistic causality

b. Internal
   4. Participation
   8. Animistic causality
   9. Dynamic causality
   12. Causality by generation
   13. Substantial identification

The data on the seventeen types of causality as outlined by Piaget were retabulated and combined into these sequence divisions. The purpose of this treatment was to see whether there were definite age relationships in the disappearance or appearance of certain kinds of causal explanations — whether the postulation of an external or an internal force began or ceased, increased or decreased, at certain ages. The data as classified by this sequence have been analyzed with respect to age, sex, and occupational groupings.

Table 14 gives the sequence classification of the answers to the question "Why does the candle go out?" as well as the materialistic classification of these same answers, which will be discussed later in this chapter. The classification numbers may be identified by reference to the explanations of the categories. (See pages 65 and 73.)

TABLE 14. — SEQUENCE AND MATERIALISTIC CLASSIFICATIONS OF ANSWERS TO QUESTION ON CANDLE IN JAR

Answer	Sequence Classification	Subdivision of Materialistic Sequence *
Oxygen necessary to burn, and it's all used up	1	1
Air used up	1	2
Smothered	2b	..
Because of the glass on top (no further explanation). .	1	5
Wholly irrelevant and inadequate. (String under cover, something smells)	1	5
No air, and necessary for burning	1	1
Oxygen all used up	1	2
Hydrogen in jar.	1	4
Air or oxygen in jar put it out	2b	..
Jar cool or damp, so put it out	1	5
Omitted	0	..
Various incorrect agents and relations. (Not enough hydrogen, smoke from candle, heat can't get out, etc.) .	1	5
Don't know	0	..
Circulation interfered with, no draft, etc..	1	4
No air, not enough air	1	2
Not enough oxygen	1	2

*For an explanation of these subdivisions see page 73.

Frequency of sequence types on individual questions. — Table 15 presents the percentage of answers to each question on both forms which are classified in each sequence category. The percentages vary considerably from question to question. The percentage in the materialistic sequence is 100 on Form II, question 3 (balloons), but only 65.8 on Form I, question 11 (connected tubes). Similarly, the percentage in the total nonmaterialistic sequence varies from zero in a number of instances to 26.4 on Form I, question 11. The percentage of answers that cannot be classified varies, likewise, from zero on Form II, question 3, to 16.6 on Form I, question 5 (color of liquids). This variation from question to question suggests again

TABLE 15. — PERCENTAGE OF ANSWERS TO EACH QUESTION FALLING INTO THE SEVERAL SEQUENCES

Question	Mate-rialistic	Nonmaterialistic			Unclassi-fiable
		Exter-nal	Inter-nal	Total	
FORM I					
Candle in jar	91.7	0.0	7.8	7.8	0.5
Penny in box	72.5	0.0	24.5	24.5	3.0
Level of water	89.2	0.0	9.4	9.4	1.4
Block dropping	84.0	0.0	10.7	10.7	5.3
Changing color of liquids. . . .	64.5	0.6	18.2	18.8	16.6
Bulb on tube	92.9	0.5	0.5	0.9	6.1
Teeter-totters.	93.2	0.0	0.0	0.0	6.8
Mixed liquids.	80.1	0.6	6.1	6.8	13.2
Paper over jar	95.3	0.0	0.0	0.0	4.7
Musical instrument	78.3	3.8	5.6	9.4	12.2
Connected tubes	65.8	10.0	16.3	26.4	7.8
All questions	82.5	1.4	9.0	10.4	7.1
FORM II					
Wind	78.6	9.9	1.0	10.9	9.5
Snow	73.8	3.7	19.0	22.8	3.4
Balloons	100.0	0.0	0.0	0.0	0.0
Carl Jenkins	79.2	6.5	0.0	6.5	14.3
Rainbow.	82.0	11.2	0.0	11.2	6.8
Airplanes	96.9	0.0	0.0	0.0	3.1
Frost.	88.1	7.5	0.0	7.5	4.4
Boats	71.4	3.1	20.1	23.1	5.4
Barns	73.8	16.3	1.0	17.3	8.8
Shadows.	99.0	0.0	0.0	0.0	1.0
Thunder	88.4	5.4	0.0	5.4	6.1
Mirror.	91.8	1.0	0.0	1.0	7.1
All questions	85.3	5.4	3.4	8.8	5.9
Both forms.	83.4	2.8	7.1	9.9	6.7

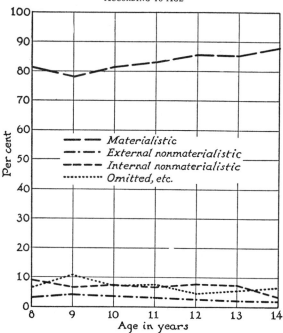

Fig. 13. — Percentage of All Answers on Forms I and II
Combined Falling in Different Sequences,
According to Age

that it is the nature of the question which determines the kind of response a child makes, and that the answers are specific to the particular question rather than related to a general level of ability in the child.

AGE, SEX, AND SOCIO-ECONOMIC TRENDS

Age changes in sequence categories. — Figure 13 presents the data on change in sequence categories according to age for Forms I and II combined. It will be seen that the age changes in this classification are very small. There is a very slight increase with age in the percentage of answers classified as materialistic — from 81.3 per cent at age 8 to 85.2 per cent at 15–16 — with the peak, 87.8 per cent, at 14. There is a slight decrease in the percentage classified as external nonmaterialistic — from 3.1 per cent at 8 to 1.6 per cent at 15–16 — though this decrease is not consistent from age to age. There is a somewhat larger decrease in internal nonmaterialistic answers, from 9.0 per cent at age 8 to 5.9 per cent at 15–16, and a

Fig. 14. — Percentage of All Answers on Forms I and II Combined Falling in Different Sequences, According to Age and Sex

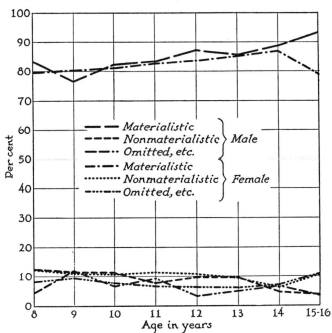

decrease in total nonmaterialistic answers from 12.1 per cent at 8 to 7.5 per cent at 15–16. There is no relationship between answers classified as "Omitted, etc.," and age.

Not much age relationship between the two types of answer could be expected, however, since even at 8 years of age a large proportion of the answers are of the materialistic type. It is interesting to note that even at the higher age levels there is an appreciable percentage

Table 16. — Percentage of All Answers Falling into the Several Sequences, According to Sex

Sequence	Boys	Girls
Materialistic	84.4	82.5
Nonmaterialistic		
External	2.1	3.4
Internal	7.2	7.0
Total	9.4	10.4
Unclassifiable.	6.2	7.1

Fig. 15. — Percentage of All Answers on Forms I and II Combined Falling in Different Sequences, According to Age and Socio-Economic Status

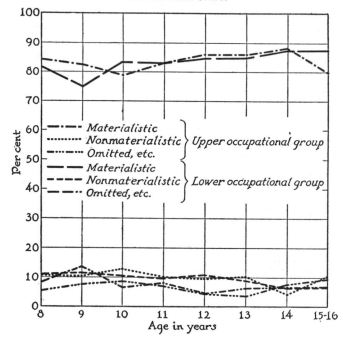

of nonmaterialistic answers — which, according to Piaget, disappear relatively early.

Sex differences in sequence classification. — Figure 14 gives the percentage of the total answers classified in three of the sequence categories, according to age and sex of the subjects. The sex differences are very small. A comparison of the percentages (all ages combined) shows practically no difference between the two sexes. Table 16 gives the percentages for the total of the two forms. The boys slightly exceed the girls, particularly at the higher age levels, in percentage of materialistic answers.

Socio-economic differences in sequence classification. — Figure 15 presents for the upper and lower occupational groupings the percentage of answers on the two forms combined which fall in three of the sequence classifications at each age. The differences are found to be very insignificant. Table 17 gives the total percentages according to occupational groupings for all ages on both forms combined. From these totals, and from the graph, it is evident that any socio-economic differences which exist are very small. The differences were more apparent on Form II than on Form I. On Form II the upper economic group consistently gave relatively more materialistic answers. This difference is in the expected direction. On Form I, however, the differences are not consistent.

TABLE 17. — PERCENTAGE OF ALL ANSWERS FALLING
INTO THE SEVERAL SEQUENCES, ACCORDING TO
OCCUPATIONAL GROUPINGS

Sequence	Upper Occupational Group	Lower Occupational Group
Materialistic	83.8	83.1
Nonmaterialistic		
External	2.1	3.2
Internal	8.1	6.5
Total	10.2	9.7
Unclassifiable.	6.0	7.2

SEQUENCE CLASSIFICATION IN RELATION TO DIFFICULTY OF QUESTIONS

Abel (1), studying unsynthetic modes of thinking among adults, found that when adults are given material of the same relative difficulty as the tasks given children, they also resort to unsynthetic thinking. Whereas Piaget found that insufficient and exaggerated syntheses of thought varied inversely with age, Abel found that they varied directly with the complexity of the material. She concludes that for every normal individual some compulsory stimulus-situation requiring logical thought will reveal limitations of memory, understanding, and communication by verbal medium, and force him to unsynthetic or prelogical modes of thought.

With these findings in mind, it was thought desirable to determine the relationship between the nonmaterialistic type of answer (which is definitely less advanced, more prelogical) and the difficulty of the question. Do children, regardless of age, turn more to the nonmaterialistic type of answer on the more difficult questions?

There were several possible criteria of the relative difficulty of the questions. One measure was found in the percentage of children who were unable to answer each question, who responded with incomplete answers or "don't know," or omitted the question entirely — all answers designated as "unclassifiable."

Another possible criterion was the mean quantified score for each question. The question upon which the children were given the highest scores would probably be the easiest, since the questions were rated with complete and correct answers as the standard.

A third criterion was based on the children's own opinions as to the difficulty of the questions, since each child had mentioned the questions which were most difficult and easiest. Accordingly, the frequency with which each question was rated as easy or hard was determined.

The rank order correlation between the percentage of nonmaterialistic answers on each question and the percentage of unclassifiable answers on that question was found to be .256. The rank order correlation between percentage of nonmaterialistic answers and the mean quantified score on that question was .269. Between percentage of nonmaterialistic answers and percentage of children who rated that question as difficult the correlation was found to be .313. As a check of the criteria, it was found that the correlation between mean quantified score on a given question and percentage of children who rated that question as difficult was .816.

Because of the large probable error of a rank order correlation involving only 23 cases, these coefficients are insignificant. It is impossible to say from these data that there is a relationship between the difficulty of the question and the type of answer (materialistic or nonmaterialistic), regardless of the age of the children.

METHOD AND PURPOSE OF MATERIALISTIC CLASSIFICATION

In the analysis of the sequence classification it was found that a very large percentage (83 per cent) of all the answers fell into the materialistic sequence. Likewise it was found that of the different Piaget types of causality which were grouped in this sequence, only three appeared with considerable frequency (phenomenistic causality, mechanical causality, and logical deduction).

When the different answers were classified into the Piaget types of causal thinking, great variation was found between types as to their inclusiveness. The greatest difficulty in classification was experienced with mechanical causality, which is very inclusive. As was seen in the Piaget analysis, nearly 40 per cent of the answers were classified in this category, and nearly 25 per cent more were classed as logical deduction. It is apparent that a classification which includes 83 per cent of the cases in three categories (phenomenistic, mechanical, and logical deduction) and leaves only about 10 per cent to be divided among ten other categories (the nonmaterialistic) is rather unanalytical. It has been noted also that there is very little age change in the materialistic sequence — necessarily so, for there is such a high percentage at the lower ages that little chance is left for increase.

Since it is reasonable to suppose that there is improvement in the type of answer with age, even in materialistic answers, it was decided to subdivide the materialistic classification. This subdivision was made on the basis of the adequacy of the answers and the type of approach to the problem — i. e., the completeness of the mechanical explanation as well as recognition of the principles involved. The definitions for the five subdivisions of the materialistic sequence are as follows:

1. Fairly complete mechanical explanation with induction of the principles involved. Correct cause-and-effect relation, with generalization of principles.

2. Fairly complete mechanical explanation without recognition of principles involved. Cause-and-effect relation presented without explanation of principles explaining this relationship.

3. Mention of principles involved in the phenomena, without tying these up to the actual mechanical explanation.

4. Incomplete mechanical explanations. No recognition of principles involved, nor indication of the causal relationship. Appeal to mechanical causes with no indication of what the cause-and-effect relationship is.

5. Phenomenalism. Two facts given together in perception, but no cause-and-effect relation given, nor any principle to explain the relationship.

By this further classification of the answers into a materialistic sequence it was hoped to discover the nature of the improvement that takes place after the child has reached the stage of development at which he gives materialistic answers. The materialistic classification is illustrated for the question "Why does the candle go out?" in Table 14. (See page 66.)

Table 18 presents for each question the percentage of the total answers in the materialistic sequence which fall into each of these five subdivisions. Considerable variation is found from question to question, as would be expected in view of the already recognized differences in difficulty. A large percentage of the answers to question 1 of Form I fall in the first subdivision, since the principle involved in the candle going out is relatively simple and is easily recognized and expressed. On the other hand, a low percentage of

TABLE 18. — PERCENTAGE OF ANSWERS FALLING INTO THE SEVERAL SUBDIVISIONS
OF THE MATERIALISTIC SEQUENCE *

Question	Subdivision				
	1	2	3	4	5
FORM I					
Candle in jar	20.2	70.4	0.0	1.4	8.0
Penny in box	0.0	8.3	12.2	6.4	73.0
Level of water	3.3	61.3	1.9	17.4	16.0
Block dropping	2.1	0.0	3.7	53.9	40.2
Color of liquids	12.9	0.0	33.8	11.7	41.6
Bulb on tube	3.5	0.2	61.9	23.4	11.0
Teeter-totters	21.0	11.3	2.5	56.9	8.3
Mixed liquids	1.0	58.2	2.9	19.6	18.2
Paper over jar	1.5	0.0	46.5	43.6	8.4
Musical instrument	0.4	1.2	1.8	48.0	48.6
Connected tubes	2.6	9.1	43.4	9.8	35.1
All questions	6.4	20.8	19.0	27.5	26.3
FORM II					
Wind	1.3	15.3	12.2	50.7	20.5
Snow	0.9	79.0	0.0	8.2	11.9
Balloons	26.5	24.5	5.1	21.1	22.8
Carl Jenkins	9.9	4.7	31.3	0.0	54.1
Rainbow	16.2	33.6	5.0	22.8	22.4
Airplanes	12.3	0.0	25.6	53.7	8.4
Frost	6.2	34.1	0.0	38.8	20.9
Boats	12.3	1.8	36.4	27.9	21.6
Barns	0.0	38.2	18.9	8.8	34.1
Shadows	13.7	11.3	12.0	53.3	9.6
Thunder	12.3	10.8	0.0	54.6	22.3
Mirror	12.6	10.0	30.5	30.8	16.0
All questions	10.9	20.8	14.9	31.9	21.5
Both forms	8.0	20.8	17.6	29.0	24.6

*For interpretation of the subdivisions see page 73.

answers is found in this first subdivision on question 2 of Form II
(What makes the snow?), because the ultimate principle which
explains the formation of snow is rather obscure, and an adequate
explanation requires more understanding and more complete verbal
command than does the principle involved in the candle going out.

AGE TRENDS IN THE MATERIALISTIC SEQUENCE

Figure 16 presents, according to the age of the children, the
percentage of answers falling into each of these subdivisions. An
inspection of this graph shows immediately that there is consider-

able change with age in the type of materialistic answer given. It will be noted that the percentage of answers of the phenomenistic type, in which no relationship exists between the phenomena mentioned and the actual phenomena, decreases markedly, from approximately 45 per cent at age 8 to slightly more than 10 per cent at 15–16. There is a considerable, though less striking, decrease in the percentage of answers of the fourth type — including mechanical explanations in which cause-and-effect relationship is not indicated.

Fig. 16. — PERCENTAGE OF ALL ANSWERS ON FORMS I AND II COMBINED FALLING INTO THE SEVERAL SUBDIVISIONS OF THE MATERIALISTIC SEQUENCE, ACCORDING TO AGE*

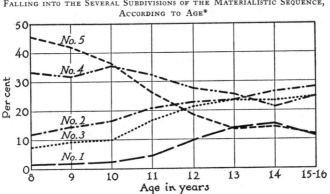

*For interpretations of the subdivisions see page 73.

This type decreases from nearly 35 per cent at age 8 to approximately 22 per cent at 15–16. There is a definite increase with age of type 3 answers, in which the principle involved in the phenomena is stated, though the actual working out of this principle, showing the cause-and-effect relationships, has not been given. This type of answer increases from about 8 per cent at age 8 to 25 per cent at the 15–16 year level. A similar increase is found in percentages of type 2, in which a fairly complete mechanical explanation is given without recognition of the principle involved, although the cause-and-effect relationship is recognized. These answers are quite adequate explanations. The percentage increases regularly from 12 at age 8 to about 18 at the 15–16-year level. The first type of explanation, that in which fairly complete mechanical explanations are given with induction of the principle involved, increases with age from a very small percentage (about 2 per cent) at the 8-year level to 11 per cent at 15–16 years, with the peak of 16 per cent at 14 years.

It is of interest to note that although there is a definite improvement with age in the type of materialistic explanation given, each of the types is represented at all age levels. We find some 8-year-old children who are capable of giving a fairly complete mechanical explanation with induction of principles; on the other hand we find a fair percentage of 15–16-year-old children still giving answers of the phenomenistic type, in which there is no causal relation between the phenomena and the material appealed to in the explanation. The overlapping is tremendous, and cautions one against classification into stages of development.

SUMMARY AND INTERPRETATION OF RESULTS

1. Piaget's 17 types of causal thinking were classified into a sequence consisting of (a) materialistic and (b) externally and internally located nonmaterialistic explanations, the purpose being to determine the age relationships, etc., between materialistic and nonmaterialistic explanations as distinct from prelogical and logical explanations.

2. There was but slight increase of materialistic explanations with age. The differences between the two sexes and between upper and lower occupational groupings were insignificant.

3. As in the Piaget sequence analysis, there was considerable variation from question to question in the percentage falling in each category. Certain questions were answered entirely by materialistic explanations; others by a fairly large percentage of nonmaterialistic answers. This is interpreted as further support for the concept of the specific nature of causal reasoning, since the manner of reasoning is found to vary with the nature of the question.

4. A large percentage (81 per cent) of the answers given at age 8 appealed to materialistic causes. This would indicate that the animistic, dynamic, prelogical type of answer has pretty well disappeared by the age of 8 years, if it ever existed, and that children at this age are not resorting to supernatural or other nonmaterialistic forces for explanations.

5. The percentage of nonmaterialistic answers to each question was related to various measures of the comparative difficulty of the questions in an attempt to determine whether children resorted to nonmaterialistic explanations when the question was too difficult for them. There were low positive correlations between difficulty and percentage of nonmaterialistic answers, indicating that within the range of these items, difficulty does not to any great extent force the children to more primitive types of causal thinking.

6. The answers classified as materialistic were subdivided into five categories on the basis of the type of explanation given, i. e., the adequacy of the explanation both in terms of cause-and-effect relationships and of the principle that is operating. Again it was found that the percentages of different types of materialistic answers vary with the specific question, indicating the specificity of causal reasoning.

7. Marked age changes were revealed by this new classification, the percentage of answers in which cause-and-effect relationships and principles were expressed increasing with age. This is evidence that after materialistic, or mechanical, reasoning has been achieved, progress is still made in the kind or level of reasoning of which the child is capable, in recognition of the cause-and-effect relationships, and in recognition of the principles underlying these relationships.

VII. ANALYSIS OF ANSWERS GIVEN BY KINDERGARTEN CHILDREN

For comparative purposes, 13 kindergarten children were given the same tests as were the children in grades 3 to 8. This group had a mean chronological age of 64.8 months, with a range of 59 to 70 months, and a mean IQ of 116.5, with a range of 103 to 130. Since it was impossible to administer the tests in the same form as that used with the older children, the individual questioning method was used. No follow-up questions were used beyond obvious repetition and slightly different wording of the same question. Any suggestion of the answer was rigidly avoided. Certain of the questions were omitted in testing these younger children because of limited time or the nature of the questions.

QUANTITATIVE ANALYSIS

Table 19 presents the percentage of the answers on each form of the test that received the several quantified scores. It will be seen that a rather large percentage of the answers given by these 5-year-

TABLE 19. — PERCENTAGE OF ALL ANSWERS OF 13 KINDER-
GARTEN CHILDREN RECEIVING EACH QUANTIFIED SCORE

Quantified Score	Form I	Form II	Forms I and II
0	20.6	16.4	18.5
1	0.0	0.0	0.0
2	2.2	0.0	1.0
3	32.6	31.8	32.5
4	17.4	40.0	30.0
5	13.0	10.0	11.5
6	14.1	0.0	6.5
7	0.0	1.8	1.0

old children received high scores — indicating that superior explanations of the phenomena are not infrequently given even at a very early age. The percentage of 0 scores is, of course, much higher than at the later ages. These consist largely of "don't know" responses.

There are rather large individual differences in the adequacy of the children's responses at this age as measured by quantified scores.

The average scores for each child on each form, and for the two forms together, are given in Table 20. The mean score for the entire group on each form and on the two forms combined was 3.16. The individual totals on the two forms range from 4.14 to 1.88 — a considerable range as compared with that for the entire group of older children. It will be noted, too, that an average score of 4.14 on

TABLE 20. — MEAN QUANTIFIED SCORES ON ALL QUESTIONS
MADE BY EACH OF 13 KINDERGARTEN CHILDREN

Child	Form I	Form II	Forms I and II
1	4.67	3.75	4.14
2	4.00	4.22	4.12
3	2.17	2.56	2.40
4	3.00	3.00	3.00
5	3.38	2.75	3.06
6	3.50	4.00	3.78
7	1.40	3.17	2.36
8	2.00	1.80	1.88
9	4.12	2.33	3.18
10	3.71	3.78	3.75
11	2.14	3.25	2.73
12	4.12	3.22	3.65
13	2.86	3.25	3.07

the two forms is halfway up the range of scores for 8- to 16-year-olds. This is a very superior performance, and much beyond what we should expect of a 5-year-old child. The child receiving this score, incidentally, was one of the youngest in the group (chronological age 62 months), and had one of the lowest IQ's (106).

QUALITATIVE ANALYSIS

Table 21 shows the percentage of these kindergarten children's answers that can be classified into each of the Piaget types of causal thinking. The outstanding features of this table are (1) the high percentage of mechanical and logical deduction answers (together totaling 25 per cent); (2) the low percentage of precausal answers (very few answers imply motivation, magic, or moral purpose, and none imply finalism, participation, or artificialistic causality); and (3) the low percentages of animistic and dynamic explanations. It would seem that the child does not resort in general to precausal explanations. If the child were pressed for an answer, it is possible that answers of a lower level might be elicited, but they are not offered spontaneously. The child does not think of phenomena in these precausal terms; he may perhaps be driven to an explanation on that level if forced to give some explanation.

TABLE 21. — PERCENTAGE OF ALL ANSWERS OF 13 KINDERGARTEN
CHILDREN FALLING INTO SEVERAL PIAGET CLASSIFICATIONS

Type of Causality	Form I	Form II	Forms I and II
1. Motivational.	2.17	0.91	1.50
3. Phenomenistic	38.04	34.55	36.50
5. Magical	0.00	14.55	8.00
8. Animistic	1.09	1.82 .	1.50
9. Dynamic	8.70	1.82	5.00
11. Mechanical	15.22	20.91	18.50
12. Generative.	0.00	6.36	3.50
16. Spatial	1.09	0.00	0.50
17. Logical	10.87	2.73	6.50
18. Trickery *	1.09	0.00	0.50
Unclassifiable	21.74	16.36	19.00

* Classification added by the present investigator.

These facts are brought out clearly in Table 22, which gives the classification of answers in the sequence analysis. It will be seen that approximately two-thirds of the answers given by these 5-year-old children appeal to some materialistic cause; about one-fifth of the answers are "don't know"; comparatively few (slightly over 19 per cent) appeal to nonmaterialistic causes.

TABLE 22. — PERCENTAGE OF ALL ANSWERS OF 13 KINDER-
GARTEN CHILDREN FALLING INTO THE SEVERAL SEQUENCES

Sequence	Form I	Form II	Forms I and II
Materialistic	66.3	58.2	61.9
Nonmaterialistic			
External	2.2	15.4	9.4
Internal	9.8	10.0	9.8
Total	12.0	25.4	19.2
Unclassifiable.	21.7	16.4	18.9

Within the materialistic sequence we find the following distribution of answers according to the classification employed in the main experiment: (1) recognition of both cause-and-effect relation and principle involved, 2.4 per cent; (2) fairly complete mechanical explanation without reference to principle, 8.8 per cent; (3) statement of principle without mechanical explanation, 0.8 per cent; (4) incomplete mechanical explanation, 28.8 per cent; and (5) phenomenalism, 59.4 per cent. Although half of the materialistic answers are of the lowest type, we do find materialistic answers of the highest type, in which both the mechanical explanation and the principle involved are given.

VIII. ITEM ANALYSIS

Comparison of Results on Specific Questions with Results of Other Investigators

Some of the items used in the two forms of this test have been used by previous investigators. A number were taken directly from Piaget's work; others were taken from Huang, Keen, Peterson, and Grigsby. Some have been used by several of these investigators. It will be of interest to compare the findings of these independent studies, in which different techniques, different ages and sampling of subjects, and different methods of analysis of data were employed.

Candle in the jar. — This item was used by Keen (23), who employed the individual testing and the multiple choice method. Keen found it to be one of the more difficult items for adolescent and older children. In the present investigation, however, this question was found to be the easiest, as determined by the mean quantified score of 6.55, which was considerably higher than that for any other item.

The kinds of answers given by the two groups are much the same. Keen notes a preponderance of items in which air is considered as burning, and few in which air is considered to be made of different substances, one of which is involved in the combustion process. A fair proportion of the answers given in the present study mention oxygen as the agent, and only a few give the impression that air itself burned. There were, however, a number of incorrect answers, involving the smoke from the candle, something about the jar, etc. All but two of the explanations offered were materialistic. These two answers involved dynamic causality.

Penny in the box. — The illustration of centrifugal force by the penny in the box has been used, with essentially the same procedure as that followed by the present investigator, by Piaget, Huang, and Keen.

Piaget found four types of answers: (1) at 6 years the borders of the box are believed to hold the penny in; (2) at 7 the child replies that the box is turning so fast the penny does not have time to fall out; (3) at 8 years the box is considered to create air which keeps the penny in position; and (4) at 9 and 10 years the box is said to displace air in the room, which produces a current that holds the penny.

Huang (19), using children up to 9 years of age, received no explanations which fall into Piaget's third and fourth types; most of his subjects from 6 to 9 gave answers of the second type (the speed of turning). His children were, therefore, less advanced than Piaget's on this item, though superior on most others. The younger children gave naïve but naturalistic explanations, often interpreting something in the perceptual field as an explanation merely because it seemed to answer the requirement.

Keen (23), working with adolescents, found that 15 per cent of the answers fell in the fourth stage (displaced air produces a current which holds the penny). Few children believed that air was created (third stage).

In the present study this item falls near the middle of the distribution as to difficulty, the mean score ranking tenth from the highest. The second-stage answer, which Piaget says is characteristic of the 7-year-old (box turns so fast the penny does not have a chance to fall out), was found to constitute 50 per cent of the answers up to age 12, and 25 per cent of the answers at ages 15 and 16. Answers such as "The sides and corners hold the penny in," "Because it didn't go upside down," and "Something holds it in" are found only at the lower end of the age range; answers such as "Centrifugal forces," "Air pressure in relation to the other side," "Too fast for gravity to act," "Force," "Friction," etc., were found exclusively at the upper end of the age range. Other answers were, however, scattered in nearly equal percentages at every age level. It becomes apparent that on this question the stages outlined by Piaget are not characteristic of limited age groups; that certain kinds of answers are given by children of all ages; and that although there is progress with age in the kind of answers given, there are no stages of development such as Piaget outlined. This question elicited more dynamic explanations than any other.

Level of water. — This item, the dropping of a pebble into a glass of water, causing the water level to rise, has been used by Zawerska (41) and Piaget (30). Zawerska found that it called forth answers varying from explanations by the succession in time of particular events to explanations based on modern scientific concepts, with a prevalence of explanations based on the idea of gravity. Piaget outlines three stages of development: (1) water is supposed to rise because the pebble is heavy, and child makes incorrect prediction when asked beforehand whether water will rise (under 7 years); (2) pebble makes water rise in proportion to its weight, though child now makes correct prediction (7–9 years); and (3) correct explanations (takes up space, heavy and goes to bottom where it takes up space, etc.) (10–11 years). Piaget finds that correct prediction precedes ability to give the reason.

In the present study the children found this problem relatively easy, as judged by the mean quantified score (rank of 3.5 among 23 questions). Almost all the answers were materialistic, the rest dynamic. The answers appearing with the greatest frequency in this age range fall into the three stages outlined by Piaget. His first stage was found to constitute 18 per cent of the answers at age 8, with scattered frequencies at other ages. Answers involving space taken up are found over the entire age range, but more often at the later ages. The answers of the older children still show confusion, however. Although a few explanations recognize that an equal volume has been displaced, many of the older children are still giving explanations such as: "Takes room of equal weight of water," "Heavy, so pushes water up," "Stone solid, nonporous." Even at the 15–16-year level there is not a clear recognition of the relation to volume.

Paper over jar. — Zawerska (41), Huang (19), and Keen (23) have used the experiment of the inverted jar of water. Zawerska reports a wide range of answers. Huang found a preponderance of naïve answers; most of the children said the paper was wet and stuck to the edge, a few referred to air as the explanation. Adults frequently mentioned wet paper sticking to the edge of the jar, and when they did mention air pressure, their understanding of the phenomenon was slight. Huang points to these answers as examples of the naïve explanations given when understanding is absent. Forty-three per cent of Keen's subjects answered that the paper was wet, sticky, etc., and 42 per cent appealed to suction.

This item was the most difficult one on the two forms, judging by the low mean quantified score. Yet there were no nonmaterialistic answers. Suction was a frequent explanation, but in this instance it was interpreted as materialistic. Answers involving sticking were found in rather large percentages at age 8, but had decreased markedly by ages 10 to 12. Explanations involving suction increased with age, but at the highest age levels were replaced by explanations involving air pressure. It is apparent, however, that even by the age of 15 or 16, few of the children had any clear idea of the true explanation of the phenomenon; and as Huang and Keen both comment, suction is employed as a term by those who have very little comprehension of what it implies.

Changing color of liquids. — Different forms of this experiment have been used by Huang and Keen. Huang (19) used colored water in red and white beakers, complicating the problem. He found that the younger children could not explain the relationship, though they recognized the correct agents, and that older children explained the appearance as due either to some coloring matter or to reflection of colors from the shades that were used. Keen (23) used flour and iodine in solution in water, to which colorless sodium thiosulphate was added. She found that the verbal expressions were characteristically precausal for both children and adults, and interprets such expressions as "the iodine being eaten up" and "the color swallowed" as merely childish expressions based on better understanding.

This question was one of the most difficult in the present study, ranking twentieth out of 23 in quantified score. Nearly all the answers were materialistic, however. A few answers of "Magic" were given at 8 to 10 years, and a few dynamic answers were scattered over the age range. A surprisingly large percentage of the children gave answers in which the explanation was attributed to an acid, a chemical, etc. This is a rather advanced form of explanation, since it implies a recognition of the kind of process at work, although the exact explanation is not given (nor can it be by most adults). Many explanations attributed the change to some specific kind of substance in the colorless liquid, which, though not correct, implied that the child understood the nature of the phenomenon. These answers were found over the whole age range. It is interesting to find that in an experiment which so definitely suggests a magical cause there are very few precausal explanations, and nearly all the explanations appeal to materialistic causes.

Bulb on tube. — This item was taken directly from Keen (23), who finds the most characteristic explanation to be in terms of suction, conceived as a force, not as absence of pressure.

This item proved fairly easy in the present study, as judged by the mean quantified score, which ranks 5.5. The explanations are all materialistic except one small group of magical answers (something said to be inside the tube), and one animistic group (tube is strong or powerful). Phenomenistic answers are fairly frequent, particularly at the earlier ages. Suction is also a frequent explanation, increasing with age up to about 12 or 13 years, when it is replaced by explanations involving more understanding, in which vacuums, air pressure, etc., play a part. This question is characterized, however, by the large percentage of the materialistic answers which give a correct statement of the principle involved, though they give no explanation of how it is worked out (62 per cent).

Block dropping. — Grigsby (11) used this item with preschool children, asking what makes the noise when the block is dropped on the table. Her findings, in general, confirm Piaget's analysis of causal thinking.

This question proved a relatively difficult one in this study, ranking sixteenth in mean quantified score. Most of the answers given were materialistic (84 per cent); a few were dynamic (10 per cent). Most of the materialistic answers fell into the fourth and fifth classifications (phenomenistic and incomplete mechanical explanations). The concept of the part played by air or air waves was not expressed until the later ages. The problem represented in this item requires too specific training for children to have mastered it. Note should be made of the fact that even where an understanding of the problem is impossible because of limited knowledge, the child has sought a materialistic and mechanical explanation rather than one in prelogical terms.

Teeter-totters. — G. M. Peterson (27) has utilized the principle of the lever in a series of twenty problems designed to measure the ability of children to generalize. His conclusion is that schooling is more closely related to generalizing ability than is age or intelligence.

In this study the experiment using teeter-totters was found to be relatively simple, the mean quantified score ranking 3.5. All the answers that were classifiable were materialistic. Subdivision of the materialistic answers shows that complete and incomplete mechanical answers comprise most of the responses, and that the two categories in which an understanding of the principle at work is involved are very small. The children, it appears, realize that the length of the arm and the size or weight of the block are involved, but have not yet reached a complete enough understanding to formulate the principles.

Boats floating. — Piaget (30) has investigated children's understanding of why boats float by verbal questioning about boats on lakes, and also by several experiments involving different-sized boats, the making of boats out of clay, and different volumes of wood and water. He finds four stages: (1) animistic and moral reasons (ends at about 5 years); (2) boats said to float because they are heavy (5–6 years); (3) boats said to float because they are light (6–8 years); and (4) recognition of true relation between weight of boat and that of the liquid element (9 years on).

In this study it was found that many of the answers given do not fit into any of these four categories. Many of the answers involve other factors — air in the boats, shape of the boats, etc. There is no clear-cut progress from one stage to the next. There are a few instances of finalism, magical causality, and dynamism, the first two types being well scattered over the entire age range and the last found only among older children. The answer that boats float because they are heavy is rare, and found in the lower half of the age range; the answer that they float because they are light is found in the same age range. Relative weight of boats and water is recognized by some children at each age level, though the percentage of answers of this type increases with age. Only one child (age 15) specifically states that the boat is lighter than an equal volume of water.

This question was relatively difficult, as judged by the mean quantified score. Only 71 per cent of the answers were classified as materialistic; 20 per cent were classified as internal nonmaterialistic.

Connected tubes. — Piaget (30) used this experiment in studying the relation of prediction to explanation. He found that discovery of laws (as determined by correct prediction) precedes discovery of correct explanations. He found three stages between the ages of 8 and 12: the first explains the rise of the water by its impetus (*élan*); the third stage is marked by correct explanation; the second stage is transitional, the prediction being correct, but the explanation still in terms of the first stage.

In the present experiment this item was found rather difficult, ranking fifteenth in mean quantified score. Only 66 per cent of the answers were materialistic; 10 per cent external nonmaterialistic; and 16.3 per cent internal nonmaterialistic. The nonmaterialistic answers included magical, finalistic, moralistic, and dynamic explanations. These are more frequently found at the earlier ages, though dynamism is found throughout the age range. Most of the materialistic answers show a recognition of the principle involved, and fall into the first and third categories of the materialistic classification. The most striking change with age is the increase in the percentage of answers in which air pressure is mentioned. Although the true relationship of air pressure to the phenomenon is not always recognized, the explanations show that it is not conceived merely as a force that does not have a mechanical explanation.

Shadows. — Piaget (32) distinguished four stages in the explanation of the phenomenon of shadows. At first they are conceived as due to the collaboration of two sources, one external and one internal (5 years); then as produced by the object alone, with a substance emanating from the object (6 and 7 years); then as formed where there is no light, but still possessing substance (8 years); finally, they are correctly explained at 9 years.

In this investigation, the explanation of shadows was relatively easy; the rank of the mean quantified score was 8. All the classifiable answers were materialistic. Fifty per cent of these answers fell in class 4 of the materialistic sequence — that is, they were incomplete mechanical explanations without recognition of the principles involved. It was found that with increasing age children are able to give a more specific statement as to the relation between light and shadows, but at all ages a large proportion of the children appreciate the fact that light (or the sun) plays the significant part in shadow formation. It is impossible from these data to find characteristic stages.

Airplanes. — Piaget (30) finds that in explaining how airplanes fly, children first dissociate themselves completely from questions of contacts and intermediaries; that in the second stage (9–11 years) the need for spatial explanation appears; and that in the third stage children realize that the airplane, to move forward, must have a supporting medium, and that that medium is the air.

Although definite stages cannot be connected with definite ages in the present study, Piaget's findings are supported in that with increasing age there is an increasing tendency for the explanations to point out the connection between agents operating to keep the airplane in the air. Instead of merely saying that the propeller makes the airplane stay up, the older children say the wind from the propeller is the cause; instead of saying air pressure keeps it up, they say air pressure under the wings keeps it up. It is apparent that with increasing age the understanding of the relationships increases.

This question ranked eleventh in mean quantified score. Every classifiable answer was materialistic.

Questions involving chance. — Two questions included in Form II of the test differ from the other items. One of these (Form II, question 4) set forth an incident in which two men with the same name were killed at the same time under similar circumstances. This item was included in order to discover what kinds of explanations children would give when confronted with a situation which had no adequate explanation, in which chance had played the major rôle. The other question (Form II, question 9) asked why a man's barn was hit four times by lightning. This item was included for a somewhat similar reason. There are several possible mechanical and logical explanations of this phenomenon. Chance does not explain it very satisfactorily, since it is unlikely that lightning would hit four times in one place. On the other hand, the current superstition that lightning never strikes twice in the same place might introduce some confusion. We wanted to discover to what extent children would turn to chance as an explanation of this phenomenon. A summary of the results follows:

Carl Jenkins. — This question (Form II, question 4) was found to be one of the most difficult for the children to explain (the mean quantified score rank was 21.5). Seventy-nine per cent of the explanations are materialistic, 6 per cent external nonmaterialistic, 14.3 per cent unclassifiable. The nonmaterialistic answers are all magical or moralistic.

It was found that there was a consistent increase in quantified score with age, and also a definite age trend in the kinds of answers given. The younger children give more answers of the phenomenistic type — that is, answers which repeat parts of the question and elaborate upon the circumstances. With increasing age there are increasing percentages of answers which recognize the chance element. Answers such as "It just happened that way," "Coincidence," "Many people have the same name," "It was accidental," etc., are found in larger percentages at the later ages. It seems that the chance element in the situation is not recognized by the younger children. There is, however, no age at which chance suddenly becomes the prevalent explanation; rather there is a very gradual increase in the percentage offering this explanation.

Barns and lightning. — This question ranked fourteenth in mean quantified score. Seventy-four per cent of the explanations were materialistic, 16 per cent external nonmaterialistic, one per cent internal nonmaterialistic, and 8.8 per cent unclassifiable. The nonmaterialistic included very small percentages of motivational, finalistic, moralistic, and animistic explanations.

The nonmaterialistic answers are found in greater frequency at the early ages, as are the answers which merely repeat parts of the problem. Answers which give plausible or probable explanations are found in greater frequency at the upper end of the age range, as are answers suggesting that the barn was struck by chance ("It just happened," "Coincidence," etc.). This suggests again that younger children do not realize the possibility of chance, though no definite conclusions should be drawn from such specific data.

Summary

A comparison of the findings obtained here with those of several investigators who have used the same questions leads to the following conclusions:

1. The actual answers given by children in the different investigations are highly similar. The answers found most frequently by one investigator are also found frequently by others when children of the same age are used as subjects.

2. There is practically no evidence supporting Piaget's classification of the answers to specific questions according to stages of development. Although no other investigator has used subjects within exactly the same age range, there is evidence that Piaget's conclusion that children of a certain age give certain typical answers is faulty. The most cogent argument against his classification is that no answer is found to be typical of a single age; that in many cases a single kind of answer is given by children over the whole age range.

3. All investigators who have repeated Piaget's questions find a much higher percentage of naturalistic answers (variously called logical, mechanical, materialistic) than Piaget reports, and find that prelogical answers such as Piaget obtains in high frequency are made conspicuous by their rarity.

4. Frequency of the use of the concept of "chance" increases with age.

IX. INTERPRETATION OF FINDINGS

INTERPRETATION OF DATA

Evaluation of the testing technique. — The technique used in this investigation, that of presenting the experiments to children in one schoolroom at a time and having them write their explanations, proved highly satisfactory. It is difficult to evaluate the technique statistically, for the usual methods of determining reliability and validity are not applicable. The reliability coefficients (odd-even) are high, however, in the opinion of the author, considering that this is not a standardized test and that every item differs greatly from every other item. The same is true of the coefficients relating one form to the other.

Several lines of evidence indicate the validity of the measure. Comparison of the answers given by these children with answers given by other children under widely different circumstances impresses one with the similarity between them. Whether the answers were elicited by the individual or the group testing method, or in one country or another, seems to make little difference in the form in which the children give their answers, in the frequency with which certain answers are found in comparison with others, or in the variety of the answers. The fact that the motivation was excellent in the group testing technique eliminates one possible criticism. Perhaps the best validation of the technique lies in the fact that when the quantified ratings given these answers are analyzed, group differences appear: there is a definite age progress in the value of the answers, and sex differences are found. If the method were not an adequate one, it is not likely that the expected age and sex relationships would be found.

There is one distinct advantage of this group testing technique over the use of the multiple choice answer technique. This advantage is that each child's answer is retained intact; and answers are not forced into four or five categories. It was found in this investigation that the answers to a single question could not be grouped into fewer than from 16 to 35 typical answers. If these answers had been forced into the four most common alternatives, the individual explanation — the one that differed from that of the majority — would have been lost. Since we were interested in a qualitative as well as a quantified analysis of the explanations, this would have defeated our purpose at the outset.

The group testing technique has an advantage over the individual testing method in that it permits the testing of a much larger number of children, thus making possible a statistical analysis of the findings and control of the sample. A major criticism of the findings of Piaget, Huang, and other investigators using the clinical method is that because their cases are few and selected, no normative conclusions can be drawn from their data. The argument might be pressed against the group method that it does not probe the depths of the child's understanding, that it accepts the first ready answer of the child as representing his best causal thinking and his actual concept. This, of course, is a possible criticism. Yet the clinical method has similar disadvantages. When a child is in face-to-face contact with an adult who is firing questions at him one after the other, he feels obliged to give some answer. Reading the accounts of certain individual interviews, in which one question follows another and the child is pressed to explain what he means by each statement, one gets the impression that the children are being driven to the wall, and that because they feel obliged to answer the questions, they invent an answer which will help them out of their difficulty. In some cases the clinical method may make more clear the completeness with which the child understands the problem, but in others it undoubtedly encourages guesswork and flights of fancy.

Piaget's classification of types of causal thinking. — Piaget's classification of children's causal thinking into seventeen types seems to have outworn its usefulness. Originally, this classification was valuable because it was a pioneer attempt to analyze causal thinking, and directed attention toward the qualitative aspects of children's explanations. In so far as this classification has stimulated further research into the nature of children's explanations, it has been valuable. The present investigation, however, has brought to light inadequacies and criticisms of the classification which suggest that it is no longer very useful as an instrument for studying children's thinking.

The experience of the judges who attempted to rate answers according to Piaget's classification gives rise to three criticisms: (1) that the types of causality as defined are vague and indefinite, making it difficult to distinguish clearly what is implied by each type, and to distinguish clearly between types; (2) that some of the answers fall outside the seventeen types as outlined by Piaget; and (3) that the interpretation of what the child really means by his answer is largely a matter of individual judgment. Three persons reading the same answer are likely to make as many different interpretations. These facts suggest that the reliability of the classification is very low, particularly when a small number of judges is used.

It was found, furthermore, when the answers had been classified, that certain types of causal thinking listed by Piaget were not represented at all in a sample of twelve thousand explanations. Apparently, these types are confined to specific questions. Other types included large percentages of the answers. These are so inclusive that they lose their analytical value.

The final criticism of the Piaget classification has been recognized by all students of the problem — that by classifying children's explanations into finalistic, moralistic, and animistic types, he is interpreting the child's world in terms of the adult conception, and reading philosophical and logical implications into the child's thoughts which may not be there at all.

Stages in the development of causal reasoning. — Throughout his discussion, Piaget implies that the development of causal thinking takes place by stages, the first stage including explanations of a phenomenistic, finalistic, magical nature; the second including artificialistic, animistic, and dynamic explanations; and the third the more truly causal explanations, with which the process of evolution is complete (at age 11 or 12). Furthermore, the answers to each specific question of causality — "What makes boats float?" "Why does the penny stay in the box?" — show stages in development that are characteristic of children of certain ages.

All the evidence in the present study points against the validity of this classification into stages. In every type of analysis — analysis of the actual answers and analysis according to Piaget's classification and according to sequence classification — the outstanding finding was the great amount of overlapping. Most kinds of answers were found over the entire age range. No kind or type of answer was found at a single age (except where the frequency was a fraction of one per cent), nor were the answers of children of a given age classifiable into a single type. The age changes in percentage of certain types of answers were gradual and in many cases negligible. It is impossible to say that certain types of answers are characteristic of children of certain ages, as distinguished from other types of answers characterizing children of other ages. Causal thinking apparently does not develop by stages but by a gradual process.

Specificity in causal thinking. — Although Piaget does not express this opinion in so many words, the impression left by his writings is that causal thinking is conceived as a general ability — that a child's thinking in general has reached a certain stage of development, and that his answers to all questions of causality involve a single type of reasoning. There is no evidence in the present study to support such an interpretation. Two types of statistical analysis point to the opposite conclusion. The first evidence is found in the relatively low odd-even and form-versus-form reliability coefficients. If the child has achieved a certain stage in the development of causal thinking, his answers to the different questions should all be on the same level, and the correlation of odd and even items should be relatively high. The second evidence is found in the striking difference between the findings on different questions. There is a wide range in mean quantified score from question to question; there is a wide range in percentage of answers to different questions that fall within the several Piaget types. Certain questions elicit one hundred per cent materialistic answers; others a much smaller percentage. Each kind of analysis shows a difference between questions. This seems to indicate that the content of the question — the nature of the phenomenon involved — directly influences the kinds of answers given. It seems evident that there is no general ability to reason causally, but rather that causal explanations are specific to the problem.

Relation of language to answers. — The part that language plays in causal reasoning has always been a debated question. Some authorities argue that the degree of understanding is limited by and equivalent to the ability to express relationships. Others maintain that understanding outstrips and precedes the ability to verbalize relationships.

Obviously, this fundamental problem has not been solved in the present experiment. One relationship between language and understanding has, however, been discovered. The correlation between quantified scores on the questions and the number of words used in the answers was found to be .45. This relationship is interpreted to mean that there is a tendency for the child who uses the most words to explain the phenomenon to be the child who best understands that phenomenon. Of course, this might not hold in individual cases.

Influence of training on causal reasoning. — Isaacs (21) criticizes Piaget's concept of maturation (which Piaget expresses in terms of the "structure" of the child's mind at different ages) on the ground that he attributes to maturation certain phenomena that can be shown to be to a real extent related to experience. Every person interested in the field has emphasized the role of experience in the development of causal reasoning. This experience is conceived in a very general sense, however, as the total of the child's contact with the environment and with cause-and-effect relationships.

Evidence presented by this study suggests that training, such as is given in the public schools, is an important factor in determining the causal explanations of children. The relationship between quantified scores and such factors as intelligence and socio-economic status, it will be remembered, was very low within a single age group, whereas the relationship between quantified scores and school grade (age held constant) was considerably higher. This suggests that the answers to these questions are more directly determined by factors involved in school experience than they are by intelligence or socio-economic status. Undoubtedly maturation and experience are limiting factors in the determination of causal thinking, but the answers to specific questions are more closely related to school experience and whatever that implies in the way of direct or indirect instruction and training.

Suggestions for Further Research

The nature of the development of children's concepts of causal relations is far from being completely understood at the present time. Each investigation suggests as many problems requiring further study as it offers tentative conclusions. Some of the problems suggested by the present study are given below:

1. More definite conclusions as to the relation of intelligence and socio-economic status to concepts of cause might be reached by the use of control groups. Four groups of children of the same age and school grade might be compared: (a) children with high intelligence and high socio-economic status; (b) children with low intelligence and high socio-economic status; (c) children with high intelligence and low socio-economic status; and (d) children with low intelligence and low socio-economic status.

2. The importance of certain experiential and tuitional factors might be revealed by more intensive study. Home interviews and questionnaires to parents might reveal other factors that have influenced the child's score. Possible related factors include the nature of the child's reading interests; the education and interests of the

parents; the types of questions asked by the child; the manner in which the adults treat the child's questions; and certain personality traits.

3. The relation between the child's verbal explanations and his ability to apply the relationships in actual situations might well be studied by the use of two carefully matched groups. One group might be given a series of situations for which they were to explain the causal relationships verbally, then presented with a similar series of situations in which the response was to be made by performance. The two series would be reversed for the second group. For example, a question on the principle of a teeter-totter, such as that asked in the present study, might be used to elicit a verbal explanation; for the performance test, the child's understanding of the principle of levers might be tested by his ability to balance the teeter-totter. Could he, by moving the fulcrum, or by choosing a block of the correct weight, demonstrate that he appreciated the relation of these factors to balance, even though he could not yet verbalize the relationship?

4. Intensive work with a few young children might contribute to our understanding of how concepts develop and help to clarify the relation between verbalization and understanding. A reasonably standardized series of situations in which the child manipulates material and experiments with the relationships would make it possible to observe the development of an understanding of the relationships and of ability to verbalize them.

5. The nature of the sex difference in causal reasoning deserves further investigation. How fundamental is this sex difference? How much is it a matter of the type of question involved? How much is it influenced by a sex difference in interest? How early does it appear? Does this sex difference persist throughout the age range and into the adult level?

SUMMARY AND CONCLUSIONS

1. By use of the group testing technique, a study was made of the development of concepts of causal relations. Two sets of questions involving causal relations were used: Form I including 11 questions preceded by demonstrations; Form II including 12 questions dealing with more general phenomena of nature, without demonstrations. Seven hundred thirty-two children between 8 and 16 years old, in grades 3 to 8, were the subjects. Seven hundred answered the questions on Form I, 335 the questions on Form II.

2. Quantified scores were determined for each answer to each question by ratings on an 8-point scale. The ratings of 13 judges as to the adequacy of the answers as scientific explanations showed high reliability. By a system of weighting, the quantified scores were made comparable from item to item.

3. The odd-even reliability of the forms (Spearman-Brown correction) were .74 and .73, respectively; the form-versus-form reliability was .534, low because of the different nature of the items on the two forms.

4. Analysis of the quantified scores revealed a consistent increase with age in the adequacy of the answers. The greatest increase was from 11 to 12 years.

5. Boys received higher quantified scores than girls, particularly on Form I, where the influence of direct training was probably less. There was but a slight relationship between quantified scores and socio-economic status as measured by occupational groupings and only a low correlation with intelligence; but there was a fairly high relation between quantified scores and school grade.

6. Analysis of the number of words used in the explanations showed considerable consistency from item to item and from form to form in the number of words used by individuals. The number of words used increased with age on Form I, not on Form II, the difference probably being due to the difference between the two forms in the nature of the items.

7. There was a slight relationship between number of words used and the socio-economic status of the child; a correlation of .35 between words used and intelligence; and a slight relationship between words used and school grade.

8. The number of words used is definitely related to the quantified score of the answer.

9. The expected sex difference in number of words used is not found. The fact that boys have higher quantified scores and that scores are related to the number of words used suggests that the superior ability of the boys to explain the questions has wiped out the expected sex difference in language usage.

10. Classification of all the answers to Piaget's seventeen types of causal thinking revealed that only four types of thinking (phenomenistic, dynamic, mechanical, and logical deduction) are found in large enough frequency to warrant further analysis.

11. There was a small sex difference in the types of answers given, boys giving slightly higher percentages of the more ad-

vanced types. Between upper and lower socio-economic groups, too, there was but a slight difference in types of explanation, though that difference was in the expected direction.

12. The overlapping between ages in types of answers was marked. No type of answer was characteristic of a single age; most types were distributed over the entire age range; and many types were found at all ages.

13. Large differences were found between the individual items on the two forms as to the percentage of each type of answer given. For example, some items elicited much higher percentages of mechanical and logical explanations than others.

14. A sub-classification was made of the seventeen types of causality, the types being divided into (1) answers involving materialistic agents and (2) answers involving nonmaterialistic agents, some external, some internal.

15. There was a slight increase with age in the percentage of answers falling into the materialistic sequence, although the percentage in this sequence was very high at all ages for all the questions. There were no sex or socio-economic differences in percentage of materialistic answers.

16. Large differences were found from item to item in the percentage of answers falling into each classification. There was very little relation, however, between the difficulty of the question and the percentage of nonmaterialistic answers.

17. The materialistic answers were subdivided into five categories in an attempt to measure changes that take place after the materialistic stage of reasoning has been reached. The categories took into consideration the adequacy of the explanation of cause-and-effect relations and of the principles involved. A striking increase of superior answers was found with advancing age, the older children giving much more nearly correct accounts of cause-and-effect relations and principles. There was a corresponding decrease with age in the percentage of phenomenistic and inadequate mechanical explanations.

18. There was a large difference between individual items in the percentage of answers falling into any one category of the materialistic classification.

19. Answers given by thirteen kindergarten children, tested individually but by the same general procedure, were analyzed. The quantified analysis showed surprisingly high scores, with many superior answers. The qualitative analysis showed that a large

percentage of the answers were of the mechanical and logical deduction types, and only a few precausal; that 62 per cent of the answers were materialistic and only 19 per cent nonmaterialistic.

20. A comparison of the items on this test with the findings of other investigators using the same items shows a striking similarity in the actual answers given in the different experiments, although fewer non-naturalistic answers are given than Piaget reports, and no evidence is found that his analysis of development into stages for individual questions is valid.

21. Two items involving "chance" factors suggest that the chance element in a situation is more frequently recognized by older than by younger children.

22. The group testing technique as used in this experiment proved very satisfactory. The evidence indicates that the reliability and validity of the technique are satisfactory. This method was found to have distinct advantages over both the multiple choice technique and the individual clinical method.

23. Piaget's classification of causal thinking into seventeen types appears to be no longer useful. The difficulty of classification, the inadequacy of the "types," and the interpretation that such a classification forces upon child thought suggest that the classification contributes little to an understanding of children's reasoning.

24. No evidence was found that children's reasoning develops by stages. Both quantified and qualitative analyses show a gradual progression in answers with advancing age, and all kinds of answers are found spread widely over the age range.

25. Evidence was found of specificity in children's causal thinking as opposed to a general level of thinking. The child responds to different questions with answers differing in qualitative as well as quantified value.

26. In this study it appears that the number of words a child uses in an explanation is in part dependent upon his understanding of the phenomenon.

27. The adequacy of the answers to these questions appears to be determined more by the tuitional or experiential factors related to schooling than by intelligence or socio-economic status. This suggests that although perhaps maturational and innate factors have a delimiting effect, specific answers are more dependent on direct or indirect instruction and training.

BIBLIOGRAPHY

1. ABEL, THEODORA MEAD. Unsynthetic modes of thinking among adults: A discussion of Piaget's concepts. American Journal of Psychology, 44:123–32 (1932).
2. BECHER, E. Untersuchung zur kindlichen Theoriebildung. Zeitschrift für Psychologie, 129:43–120. Abstracted in Psychological Abstracts, 7:667 (November, 1933). Abstract No. 5469.
3. BEDELL, R. C. The relationship between the ability to recall and the ability to infer in special learning situations. Science Education, 18:158–62 (1934).
4. BURT, CYRIL. The development of reasoning in school children. Journal of Experimental Pedagogy, 5:68–77 (1919).
5. CHANT, S. N. F. An objective experiment on reasoning. American Journal of Psychology, 45:282–91 (1933).
6. DAVIS, EDITH A. Form and function of children's questions. Child Development, 3:57–74 (1932).
7. DAY, ELLA J. The development of language in twins. I. A comparison of twins and single children. Child Development, 3:179–99 (1932).
8. DECROLY, O. Études de psychogénèse. Observations, expériences, et enquêtes sur le développement des aptitudes de l'enfant. Brussels, 1932. 348 pp. Abstracted in Psychological Abstracts, 7:668 (November, 1933). Abstract No. 5476.
9. GOODENOUGH, FLORENCE L., and JOHN E. ANDERSON. Experimental child study. The Century Co., New York, 1931. ix + 546 pp.
10. GREEN, HELEN J., and others. A manual of selected occupational tests for use in public employment offices. Bulletins of the Employment Stabilization Research Institute, University of Minnesota, Vol. 2, No. 3. Minneapolis, University of Minnesota Press, 1933.
11. GRIGSBY, OLIVE JOHN. An experimental study of the development of concepts of relationship in preschool children as evidenced by their expressive ability. Journal of Experimental Education, 1:144–62 (1932).
12. GUILLET, C. The growth of a child's concepts. Pedagogical Seminary, 24: 81–96 (1917).
13. HARRISON, M. L. The nature and development of concepts of time among young children. Elementary School Journal, 34: 507–14 (1934).
14. HAZLITT, V. Children's thinking. British Journal of Psychology, 87:447–531 (1930).
15. HEIDBREDER, EDNA. Problem solving in children and adults. Journal of Genetic Psychology, 35:522–45 (1928).
16. ——— Reasons used in solving problems. Journal of Experimental Psychology, 10:397–414 (1929).
17. ——— A study of the evolution of concepts. Psychological Bulletin, 31:673 (1934). Abstract.
18. HERZFELD, E., and K. WOLF. Quoted in Charlotte Bühler, Kindheit und Jugend. Hirzel, Leipzig, 1928. 204 pp.
19. HUANG, I. Children's explanations of strange phenomena. Smith College Studies in Psychology, No. 1, 1930. 180 pp.
20. ILLGE, W. Das Kind und das Unfassbare. Zeitschrift für päd. Psychologie, 31:410–17. Abstracted in Psychological Abstracts, 6:460 (September, 1932). Abstract No. 3714.

21. ISAACS, SUSAN. Intellectual growth in young children. Harcourt, Brace, and Co., New York, 1930. xi+370 pp.
22. JOHNSON, E. C., and C. C. JOSEY. A note on the development of thought forms of children as described by Piaget. Journal of Abnormal and Social Psychology, 26:338–39 (1931).
23. KEEN, ANGELINE M. A study of the growth of concepts and of reasoning concerning physical and psychological causation. Ph.D. thesis, 1934, on file in the University of California Library, Berkeley, California. 111 pp.
24. LABRANT, LOU L. Studies of certain language development of children in grades 4 to 12, inclusive. Genetic Psychology Monographs, 14:387–491 (1933).
25. MCCARTHY, DOROTHEA M. The language development of the preschool child. University of Minnesota Institute of Child Welfare Monographs, No. 4. Minneapolis, University of Minnesota Press, 1930. 174 pp.
26. MEAD, MARGARET. An investigation of the thought of primitive children with special reference to animism. Journal of the Royal Anthropological Institute of Great Britain and Ireland, 62:173–90 (1932).
27. PETERSON, GEORGE M. An empirical study of the ability to generalize. Journal of General Psychology, 6:90–114 (1932).
28. PIAGET, JEAN. La causalité chez l'enfant. British Journal of Psychology, 18:276–301 (1928).
29. ——— The child's conception of the world. Harcourt, Brace, and Co., New York, 1929. ix+397 pp.
30. ——— The child's conception of physical causality. Harcourt, Brace, and Co., New York, 1930. viii + 309 pp.
31. ——— Judgment and reasoning in the child. Harcourt, Brace, and Co., New York, 1928. vii+257 pp.
32. ——— The language and thought of the child. Harcourt, Brace, and Co., New York, 1926. vii+246 pp.
33. RASPE, C. Kindliche Selbstbeobachtung und Theoriebildung. Zeitschrift angewandte Psychologie, 23:302–28 (1924).
34. SANDER, F. Ganzheit und Gestalt; psychologisch Untersuchungen. V. Lichtenberger, W. Ueber das physikalisch-kausale Denken bei Hilfsschülern. Archiv für die gesamte Psychologie, 87:447–531 (1933). Abstracted in Psychological Abstracts, 7:586 (October, 1933). Abstract No. 4779.
35. SHAFFER, LAURANCE F. The measurement of the child's concepts. Journal of Educational Psychology, 19:41–44 (1928).
36. SMITH, MADORAH. An investigation of the development of the sentence and the extent of vocabulary in young children. University of Iowa Studies in Child Welfare, Vol. 3, No. 5, 1926. 92 pp.
37. TWO PARENTS. The scientific interests of a boy in preschool years. Forum of Education, 6:17–37 (1928).
38. WINCH, W. H. Children's reasonings: experimental studies of reasoning in school children. Journal of Experimental Pedagogy, 6:121–41 (1921).
39. ——— Children's reasonings. Journal of Experimental Pedagogy, 6:199–212 (1922).
40. ——— Children's reasonings: An experimental study of reasoning in school children. Forum of Education, 1:152–57 (1923).
41. ZAWERSKA, J. Wyjasnianie zjawisk przyrodniczych przez dzieci. Polskie Archives Psychologie, 3:110–27 (1930). Abstracted in Psychological Abstracts, 6:464 (September, 1932). Abstract No. 3739.
42. ZEININGER, K. Magische Geisteshaltung ins Kindersalter und ihre Bedeutung für die religiöse Entwicklung. Beihefte zur Zeitschrift angewandte Psychologie, No. 47, p. 155 (1929).

INDEX

Date Due